easy pasta

2016

easy pasta

simple recipes for great-tasting pasta

RYLAND
PETERS
& SMALL

LONDON NEW YORK

Senior Designer Toni Kay
Editor Delphine Lawrance
Picture Research Emily Westlake
Production Controller Maria Petalidou
Art Director Leslie Harrington
Publishing Director Alison Starling

First published in the United Kingdom
in 2010 by Ryland Peters & Small
20–21 Jockey's Fields
London WC1R 4BW
www.rylandpeters.com

10 9 8 7 6 5 4 3 2 1

Text © Fiona Beckett, Maxine Clark, Ross Dobson,
Clare Ferguson, Tonia George, Brian Glover, Nicola
Graimes, Jennifer Joyce, Caroline Marson, Louise
Pickford, Fiona Smith, Fran Warde, Laura Washburn,
Lindy Wildsmith and Ryland Peters & Small 2010

Design and photographs
© Ryland Peters & Small 2010

ISBN: 978-1-84597-960-7

A CIP record for this book is available from the
British Library.

Printed and bound in China

contents

introduction

More than 100 recipes are included in this handy book to inspire you to bring a taste of Italy to the table; many have suggested variations to help you make the best of what's in season or in your pantry.

Learn which pasta shape works best with which type of sauce and even how to make your own pasta. It's a surefire way to impress guests and much easier to make than you might think. It also gives you carte blanche to create any shape you like.

Most of the recipes are based on using dried pasta but feel free to substitute for fresh pasta. Supermarkets today offer such a wide choice that it seems a shame not to. Just be sure to reduce the cooking time.

The recipes are divided into six sections, beginning with pasta soups and salads then moving on to meat and poultry, fish and seafood, vegetables and herbs, cream and cheese and lastly, hearty pasta bakes. The only difficulty you'll have is choosing which recipe to make!

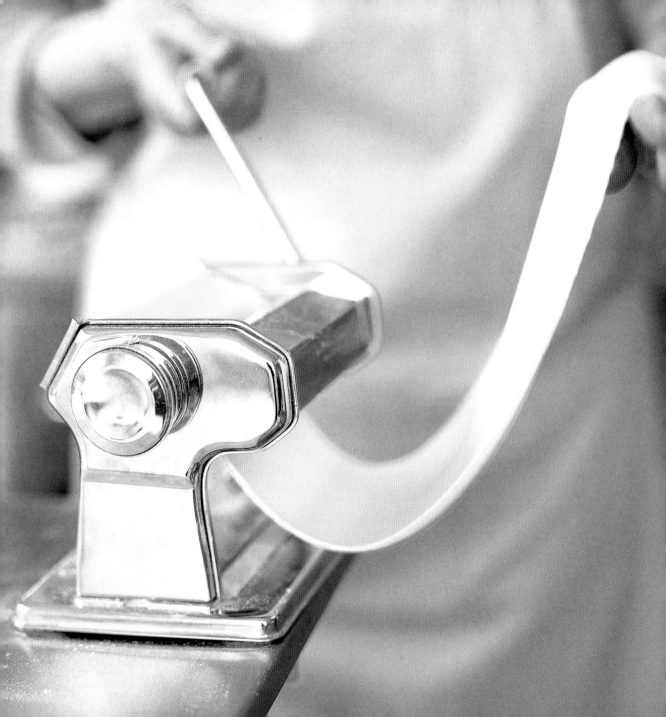

choosing and making pasta

dried pasta types

Pasta comes in a huge range of shapes, sizes and lengths, falling into the basic categories of strands, ribbons, tubes and shapes. Which one you choose will depend mainly on the sauce you are serving with your pasta. Strands (such as spaghetti) and ribbons (such as fettuccini) are ideal with light and oil-based sauces, which coat the strands evenly. Tubes (such as penne) or shapes (such as conchiglie) go well with chunky or meaty sauces, as their insides catch the sauce. But these are just guidelines, not a set of rules – you should choose pairings that you like or that simply suit your mood.

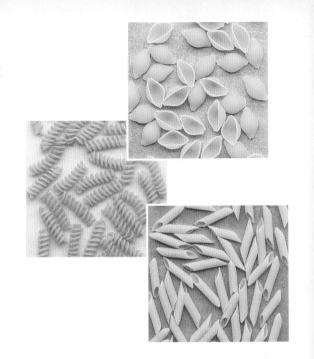

STRANDS AND RIBBONS

Long pasta, known as 'pasta lunga', comes either as long strands (hollow or solid) or as flat ribbons, called 'fettucce'.
Strands: spaghetti, spaghettini, bucatini – which are hollow.
Ribbons: tagliatelle, linguine, tagliolini, fettuccine, pappardelle.

TUBES AND SHAPES

Tubes and shapes are either plain or ridged – 'rigati'. The ridges help the sauce cling to the pasta.
Tubes: penne, chifferi, rigatoni, macaroni.
Shapes: fusilli, conchiglie, farfalle, orecchiette, gemelli.

PASTA FOR SOUPS

Very small shapes are ideal for soups, as they look very pretty and delicate and don't dominate the soup.
Soup pasta: anellini, fedelini, stelline, alfabetini, ditali.

PASTA FOR BAKING

Lasagne are flat sheets of pasta, layered with sauce in baked dishes. Cannelloni are large tubes for stuffing and baking.

FLAVOURED PASTA

Pasta flavoured and coloured with spinach, tomato or squid ink are the most common, although beetroot, basil and saffron flavour are also available in many shops.

pairing sauces with pasta

Given the variety of sauces and the similar abundance of pasta types and shapes that are available, it can often be difficult to choose which sauce to combine with which type of pasta. Although the choice is very much down to the individual, here are some handy tips to help you on your way to creating a combination that would make the Italians proud.

Some sauces take no time at all to prepare, involve very little cooking and are more like dressings than sauces. In fact, the word condimento (dressing) comes to mind; the Italians often use it rather than salsa or sugo (sauce) when talking about pasta. Other sauces, particularly meat sauces, can be prepared in advance (a plus when having friends over), then reheated when required. Many have store-cupboard equivalents, which are great for unexpected guests and 'home-from-work, straight-onto-the-table' meals. All are easy to make – the choice is yours.

WHICH SAUCE FOR WHICH PASTA?

Homemade pasta made with eggs and wheat flour comes from the north of Italy. The sauces that are served with it are, on the whole, rich meat- and dairy-based sauces enhanced with Parmesan cheese, reflecting the rich agricultural heritage of the north. Spaghetti made with durum wheat flour, cultivated in the more arid south, comes originally from Naples. Myriad homemade pasta shapes, made with this flour, water and the spirit of invention brought by necessity, are set in the traditions of the cooking of the south.

There is a simple rule to follow when deciding which pasta to serve with which sauce. Egg pasta, long or short, is perfect for sauces based on dairy food and meat, while spaghetti and other pasta shapes made with durum wheat are more suited to the lighter, olive-oil-based sauces made with fish and vegetables.

Cream and meat sauces also go well with ridged tubes, especially if there are small delicious bits to get trapped inside. Ridged pasta is particularly good for creamy sauces, as the sauce binds itself to the ridges.

One last word – don't be afraid to try different sauces with different pastas and find out what you like!

making basic pasta dough

200 g Italian '00' flour or 100 g Italian '00' flour and 100 g Farina di Semola

2 medium eggs

1 tablespoon olive oil

a pinch of sea salt and freshly ground black pepper

MAKES APPROXIMATELY 500 G

Nothing beats homemade pasta – not even shop-bought 'fresh'. A mixture of 50% Italian '00' flour and 50% Farina di Semola (pale yellow, finely ground, hard durum wheat flour for making pasta and some breads – fine Farola baby food is semolina flour) works particularly well. This mixture of soft and hard wheat flours gives the dough a firmer texture. You may also use strong white bread flour. The dough must not be too soft – it should require some serious effort when kneading! However, too much extra flour will make the pasta too tough to handle (or put through the pasta machine) and when cooked, taste floury. Generally allow one egg to 100 g flour per portion for a main course. It's best to make a large batch in one go and freeze it once cut and shaped.

To make the pasta in the traditional way, sift the flour onto a clean work surface and make a well in the centre with your fist.

(**1**) Break the eggs into the well and add a pinch of salt and freshly ground black pepper and the oil.

(**2**) Gradually mix the eggs into the flour with the fingers of one hand, and bring it together into a firm dough. If the dough feels too dry, add a few drops of water; if too wet, add more flour. You will soon grow accustomed to how the dough should feel once you've made it a few times.

(**3**) Knead the pasta until smooth, lightly massage it with a hint of olive oil, pop into a plastic food bag and allow to rest for at least 30 minutes before attempting to roll out. The pasta will be much more elastic after resting.

(**4**) Roll out by hand with a long wooden rolling pin or use a pasta machine (see page 15).

Tip The Italian way is ALWAYS to toss the cooked, hot pasta with the sauce before serving.

using a pasta machine

Feed the rested dough 4–5 times through the widest setting of a pasta machine, folding into three each time, and feeding the open ends through the rollers to push out any air. This will finish the kneading process and make the pasta silky smooth.

Next, pass the pasta through the machine, starting at the widest setting first, then reducing the settings, one by one, until reaching the required thickness. The pasta sheet will become very long – so if you are having trouble, cut it into two and feed each half through separately.

Generally the second-from-last setting is best for tagliatelle; the finest is for ravioli or pasta that is to be filled.

Once the required thickness is reached, hang the pasta over a broom handle or the back of a chair to dry a little – this will make cutting it easier in humid weather, as it will not be so sticky. Alternatively, dust with a little flour and lay out on clean tea towels.

Next, pass the pasta through the chosen cutters (tagliolini, tagliatelle, etc) then drape the cut pasta over the broom handle again to dry further, until ready to cook. Alternatively, toss the cut pasta lightly in flour (preferably semolina flour) and lay out in loose bundles on a tray lined with a clean tea towel. Use as soon as possible before it sticks together.

making pasta shapes by hand

Tagliatelle Roll the dough out thinly on a lightly floured surface or using a pasta machine. (**1**) Roll or fold one end loosely towards the centre of the sheet, then do the same with the other so that they almost meet in the middle. Lift one folded side on top of the other – do not press down on the fold. (**2**) Working quickly and deftly with one motion, cut into thin slices with a sharp knife, down the length of the folded pasta. (**3**) Immediately unravel the slices (or they will stick together) to reveal the pasta ribbons – you can do this by inserting the back of a large knife and shaking them loose. Hang to dry a little before cooking or (**4**) dust well with semolina flour and arrange in loose 'nests' on a tray lined with a clean tea towel.

Pappardelle Roll the dough out thinly on a lightly floured surface or using a pasta machine. Using a fluted pastry wheel, cut into wide ribbons. Hang up to dry a little before cooking.

Tortellini Roll the dough out thinly on a lightly floured surface or using a pasta machine. Using a round biscuit cutter, stamp out rounds of pasta. Pipe or spoon your chosen filling into the middle of each round. Brush the edges with beaten egg and carefully fold the round into a crescent shape, excluding all air. Bend the two corners round to meet each other and press well to seal. Repeat with the remaining dough. Leave to dry on a floured tea towel for about 30 minutes before cooking.

Ravioli Halve the dough and wrap one half in clingfilm. Roll the pasta out thinly on a lightly floured surface or using a pasta machine. Cover with a clean tea towel or clingfilm and repeat with the rest of the dough. Pipe or spoon small mounds (about 5 ml/1 teaspoon) of filling in even rows, spacing them at 4-cm intervals across one piece of the dough. Using a pastry brush, brush the spaces of dough between the mounds with beaten egg. Using a rolling pin, lift the remaining sheet of pasta over the mounds. Press down firmly between the pockets of filling, pushing out any trapped air. Cut into squares with a serrated ravioli/pastry cutter or sharp knife. Transfer to a floured tea towel to rest for about 1 hour before cooking.

flavouring and cooking pasta

Spinach pasta Follow the Basic Pasta Dough recipe (see page 12). Sift the flour onto a clean work surface. Next, blend the flour with 150 g frozen leaf spinach (cooked and squeezed to remove as much moisture as possible), a pinch of salt, some pepper and 2 medium eggs, until

very smooth, and continue as per the Basic Pasta Dough method, from point (**3**).

Tomato pasta Add 2 tbsp (tablespoons) tomato purée or sun-dried tomato paste to the well in the flour. Use 1 large egg instead of 2 medium ones.

Beet pasta Add 2 tbsp grated cooked beetroot to the well in the flour. Use 1 large egg instead of 2 medium ones.

Saffron pasta Soak a sachet of powdered saffron in 2 tbsp hot water for 15 minutes. Use 1 large egg instead of 2 medium ones and whisk in the saffron water.

Herb pasta Add at least 3 tbsp finely chopped fresh green herbs to the well in the flour. Or blanch the herbs, dry, then chop before the time comes to use them.

Black squid ink pasta Add 1 sachet of squid ink to the eggs before adding to the flour. A little extra flour may be needed.

How to cook Cooking times for fresh and dried pasta vary according to the size and quality of the pasta. The only way to check is to taste it (and to follow the packet instructions). However, the basic method of cooking remains the same. Wholemeal

pasta will always take a little longer to cook than white pasta.

Throw the pasta into a large saucepan of boiling, salted water – as a guide, you will need about 4 litres water and 3 tbsp salt for every 375–500 g fresh or dried pasta. It is this large volume of water that will prevent the pasta from sticking together. Stir once or twice – if you have enough water in the pan and you stir the pasta as it goes in, it shouldn't stick. DO NOT COVER, or the water will boil over. Quickly bring the pasta back to a rolling boil, stir and boil until it is 'al dente', or firm to the bite. It should not have a hard centre or be soggy and floppy. Calculate the cooking time from the moment the pasta starts to boil again and have a colander to hand for draining.

Next, drain the pasta, holding back 2–3 tbsp of the cooking water, returning the pasta to the pan (the dissolved starch in the water helps the sauce cling to the pasta). Dress the pasta straight away with the sauce directly in the pan. Serve immediately.

pasta soups and salads

summer minestrone

50 g small dried pasta shapes, such as anellini or fedelini

1 tablespoon olive oil

1 red onion, chopped

1 garlic clove, finely chopped

2 celery stalks, thinly sliced

150 g baby carrots, thinly sliced

2 plum tomatoes, coarsely chopped

1.25 litres vegetable stock

150 g runner beans, thinly sliced

2 tablespoons fresh Pesto (page 163)

sea salt and freshly ground black pepper

freshly grated Parmesan cheese, to serve

SERVES 4

This is a very light, fragrant version of a soup that can sometimes be rather heavy. It has added sparkle thanks to the last-minute addition of fresh pesto.

Bring a large saucepan of salted water to the boil. Add the pasta and cook until al dente, or according to the instructions on the packet. Drain well.

Meanwhile, heat the oil in another large saucepan, add the onion and garlic and cook gently for 3 minutes. Add the celery and carrots and cook for a further 2 minutes. Add the tomatoes and cook for 2 minutes.

Add the stock and beans, bring to a boil, then simmer for 5–10 minutes, until the vegetables are cooked and tender.

Add the drained pasta, stir in the pesto, and season to taste. Divide between 4 bowls, sprinkle with Parmesan, then serve.

conchigliette soup

1 tablespoon olive oil

1 onion, finely chopped

2 garlic cloves, finely chopped

2 red chillies, thinly sliced into rings

4 slices smoked streaky bacon, finely chopped

1 teaspoon fresh marjoram or oregano

400 g tinned artichoke hearts in water, drained and quartered

100 g frozen peas

1.25 litres chicken stock

75 g dried pasta shapes, such as conchigliette or gnocchetti

sea salt and freshly ground black pepper

freshly grated Parmesan cheese, to serve

SERVES 4

An incredibly speedy soup that has a wonderful, fresh flavour, yet is made almost entirely from ingredients found in the store-cupboard. Enjoy a taste of summer all year round.

Heat the oil in a large saucepan, add the onion, garlic, chillies and bacon, and cook for 4–5 minutes until golden.

Add the marjoram or oregano, artichokes and peas and stir-fry for 2 minutes. Add the stock, bring to a boil, then simmer for 10 minutes.

Meanwhile, bring a large saucepan of salted water to the boil. Add the pasta and cook until al dente, or according to the instructions on the packet.

Drain the pasta and add it to the soup. Season the soup to taste and divide between 4 bowls. Sprinkle with Parmesan, then serve.

2 tablespoons olive oil

1 small onion, finely chopped

2 garlic cloves, finely chopped

1 potato, diced

2 ripe tomatoes, coarsely chopped

1.25 litres chicken or vegetable stock

a sprig of thyme, sage or rosemary

800 g tinned cannellini beans, drained

150 g small dried pasta shapes,
such as orecchiette

a pinch of crushed dried chillies

sea salt and freshly ground
black pepper

freshly grated Parmesan cheese,
to serve

SERVES 4

This hearty soup of pasta and beans is a classic
from the region of Puglia in Italy – the pasta shapes
traditionally used are orecchiette, meaning 'little ears'.

pasta e fagioli

Heat the oil in a large saucepan, add the onion, garlic and potato
and cook for 3–4 minutes until golden. Add the tomatoes and cook
for 2–3 minutes until softened.

Add the stock, herbs, beans, pasta, dried chillies, salt and pepper.
Bring to the boil, then simmer for about 10 minutes, until the pasta
and potatoes are cooked.

Divide between 4 bowls, sprinkle with Parmesan, then serve.

500 ml fresh chicken stock

250 ml dry white wine

1 small onion, sliced

1 celery stick, cut into 3 pieces

1 bay leaf

2 slices unwaxed lemon

8–10 black peppercorns

4 chicken breasts (about 600 g)

200 g dried egg pasta shapes

8 halved artichoke hearts (optional)

1 tablespoon roughly chopped
flat leaf parsley

dressing

100 g tinned premium tuna, drained

2 tablespoons capers, rinsed

2 tablespoons lemon juice

3 tinned or bottled anchovy fillets,
rinsed and finely chopped

200 g good-quality mayonnaise

a pinch of cayenne pepper

gremolata

5–6 tinned or bottled anchovy fillets,
rinsed and chopped

2 spring onions, thinly sliced

grated zest of 1 small unwaxed lemon

1 tablespoon small capers

3 tablespoons chopped
flat leaf parsley

salad leaves and tomatoes, to serve

SERVES 6

This is a really easy yet impressive pasta salad. Don't be daunted by the rather long list of ingredients – the gremolata is based on pretty much the same ingredients as the dressing, but roughly chopped.

chicken tonnato salad

Pour the stock and wine into a large saucepan that is big enough to hold the chicken breasts in a single layer. Bring to the boil, add the onion, celery, bay leaf, lemon and peppercorns and simmer for 5 minutes. Carefully lower the chicken breasts into the stock, adding some boiling water, if needed, to cover them. Bring back to the boil, then turn the heat right down and simmer very slowly for another 5 minutes. Turn the heat off, cover the pan and let the chicken cool in the stock. (This will take about 4–5 hours.)

Once the chicken is cool, make the dressing. Put the tuna in a food processor with the capers, lemon juice and anchovy fillets and whizz until you have a paste. Add the mayonnaise and cayenne pepper and whizz again until smooth. Turn into a large bowl. Put all the ingredients for the gremolata in another bowl and mix them together to combine.

Bring a large saucepan of salted water to the boil. Add the pasta and cook until al dente, or according to the instructions on the packet. Refresh with cold water.

Remove the chicken from the poaching liquid and cut into rough chunks. Add the chicken, pasta and gremolata to the dressing and toss lightly. Check the seasoning, adding more lemon juice or cayenne pepper to taste (you shouldn't need salt).

To assemble, arrange a handful of salad leaves on each plate, scatter over a few tomatoes, then spoon the salad on top. Arrange the artichoke hearts, if using, over the top and sprinkle with the roughly chopped parsley.

tuna and coriander pasta salad

500 g dried pasta, such as tagliatelle, conchiglie or farfalle

tomato salad

4 firm tomatoes

3 tablespoons olive oil

1½ tablespoons chopped mint or flat leaf parsley

sea salt and freshly ground black pepper

sauce

2 tablespoons olive oil

2 onions, thinly sliced

1 teaspoon crushed coriander seeds

160 g tinned tuna in oil, lightly drained

1½ tablespoons capers (optional)

grated zest of 1 unwaxed lemon

125 ml milk

sea salt and freshly ground black pepper

a handful of mint sprigs, to serve

SERVES 4–6

This is a delicious lunch or supper dish made with ingredients that, although not all strictly from the store-cupboard, are to be found in most kitchens.

Bring a large saucepan of salted water to the boil. Add the pasta and cook until al dente, or according to the instructions on the packet. Refresh with cold water.

For the salad, cut a cross in the top and bottom of the tomatoes, then plunge them briefly into boiling water. Drain, pull off the skins, then remove the seeds and cores. Cut into small cubes. Add the oil and mint. Season to taste and set aside to develop the flavours.

To make the sauce, heat the oil in a frying pan set over medium heat. Add the onions and coriander seeds and cook slowly. When the onions start to soften, add 3 tablespoons water and cover with a lid. Continue cooking over low heat until soft. This will take 15 minutes – do not rush (add extra water if necessary).

When the onions are very soft, add the tuna, capers, if using, lemon zest, some salt, lots of pepper and half the milk. Stir well, cover again and cook for 10 minutes over low heat (add the remaining milk if necessary).

Add the sauce and the tomato salad to the pasta and mix well. Sprinkle with mint sprigs and serve at once.

Variation Substitute 300 g halved cherry tomatoes for the salad.

Here, a number of typically Mediterranean flavours are served with wholemeal pasta. The feta cheese adds a lovely sharp tang. Using wholemeal pasta instead of white not only gives a nuttier taste, it also lowers this salad's glycaemic index.

pepper, olive and feta pasta salad

1 red pepper

1 yellow pepper

3 tablespoons olive oil

2 teaspoons thyme leaves

1 tablespoon roughly chopped flaf leaf parsley

1 handful of small basil leaves

80 g kalamata olives, halved

400 g dried wholemeal penne or similar pasta

150 g feta cheese, crumbled

sea salt and freshly ground black pepper

SERVES 4

Preheat the oven to 220°C (425°F) Gas 7. Brush the peppers with 1 tablespoon of the oil, place in a roasting tin and cook in the oven for 15 minutes, turning often until they puff up and blacken evenly all over.

Remove the peppers from the oven and place them in a plastic food bag. When cool enough to handle, remove the skin, stalks, seeds and any membranes and thinly slice the remaining flesh. Put the slices in a large bowl and add the remaining oil, the herbs and olives. Cover and set aside for around 30 minutes to allow the flavours to develop.

Bring a large saucepan of salted water to the boil. Add the pasta and cook until al dente, or according to the instructions on the packet. Rinse under cold water, drain and add to the other ingredients. Use your hands to mix well. Season with salt and pepper, add the feta and toss again before serving.

pea, prosciutto and pasta salad

350 g dried pasta shapes of your choice, such as orecchiette or fusilli

1 tablespoon olive oil

1 large onion, finely chopped

2 garlic cloves, crushed

100 g sliced prosciutto or bacon rashers

350 g frozen or fresh peas

2 tablespoons extra virgin olive oil

2 tablespoons white wine vinegar

1 teaspoon Dijon mustard

2 tablespoons chopped parsley

2 tablespoons chopped chervil

2 tablespoons chopped mint

sea salt and freshly ground black pepper

SERVES 6

This is an elegant and light twist on a traditional pasta salad. You can either use frozen peas or make the most of the tender sweetness of fresh peas when they are in season; as a rule of thumb, 500 g pea pods will yield about 175 g fresh peas.

Bring a large saucepan of salted water to the boil. Add the pasta and cook until al dente, or according to the packet instructions.

Meanwhile, heat the oil in a frying pan set over medium heat. Add the onion and garlic and cook for 5 minutes. Next, add the prosciutto and cook for a further 5 minutes. Finally, add the peas, cover and cook gently for 5 minutes until they are tender. (Remember that fresh peas will need slightly less cooking.)

For the vinaigrette, mix together the extra virgin olive oil, vinegar and mustard in a bowl, adding salt and pepper to taste.

When the pasta is cooked, drain and refresh with cold water to cool a little. Combine the pasta with the pea and prosciutto mixture, vinaigrette, parsley, chervil and mint.

tuna, chilli and rocket pasta salad with feta

400 g large dried pasta shells, such as lumaconi

65 ml olive oil

2 red onions, finely chopped

2 garlic cloves, finely chopped

1 large red chilli, deseeded and finely chopped

2 tablespoons small salted capers, rinsed

1 tablespoon red wine vinegar

400g tinned tuna chunks in oil, well drained

50 g feta cheese, crumbled

50 g rocket

sea salt and freshly ground black pepper

lemon wedges, to serve

SERVES 4

Any large, open pasta shape will work, but I have used lumaconi here, which translated from the Italian means 'big snail shells'.

Bring a large saucepan of salted water to the boil. Add the pasta and cook until al dente, or according to the instructions on the packet. Drain well and add 1 tablespoon of the oil. Transfer to a large bowl.

Heat the remaining oil in a large frying pan set over high heat. Add the onions, garlic, chilli and capers and cook, stirring, for 2–3 minutes, until the onion has softened. Add the vinegar and cook for another minute. Add the tuna and use a fork to roughly break up any larger chunks, without mushing the tuna too much.

Add the tuna mixture to the bowl with the pasta. Add the feta and rocket and gently toss to combine. Season to taste with salt and a generous amount of pepper. Serve warm or cold, as desired, with lemon wedges for squeezing.

butternut squash and feta pasta salad

750 g butternut squash

1 tablespoon extra virgin olive oil

1 tablespoon chopped thyme leaves

500 g dried penne

350 g feta cheese, diced

350 g cherry tomatoes, halved

4 tablespoons chopped basil

4 tablespoons pumpkin seeds, toasted in a dry frying pan

sea salt and freshly ground black pepper

dressing

150 ml extra virgin olive oil

3 tablespoons tapenade

freshly squeezed juice of 1 lemon

1 teaspoon clear honey

sea salt and freshly ground black pepper

SERVES 6

The sweetness of the butternut squash combines wonderfully with the sharpness of the feta cheese, while the pumpkin seeds add a little crunchy goodness to this hearty pasta salad.

Preheat the oven to 200°C (400°F) Gas 6.

Peel and deseed the butternut squash and cut the flesh into bite-sized pieces. Put into a bowl or plastic bag, then add the oil, thyme, salt and pepper. Toss well, then arrange in a single layer in a roasting tin. Roast in the preheated oven for about 25 minutes until golden and tender. Leave to cool.

To make the dressing, put the oil, tapenade, lemon juice and honey into a bowl. Whisk well, then add salt and pepper to taste.

Bring a large saucepan of salted water to the boil. Add the pasta and cook until al dente, or according to the instructions on the packet. Drain well, then immediately stir in 4 tablespoons of the dressing. Leave to cool.

When cool, put the pasta and squash into a salad bowl and mix gently. Then add the feta cheese, tomatoes, basil and toasted pumpkin seeds. Just before serving, stir in the remaining dressing.

lemon-rubbed lamb and orzo salad

3 garlic cloves, crushed

finely grated zest of 2 unwaxed lemons and freshly squeezed juice of 1

3 tablespoons olive oil

300-g piece of lean lamb fillet

1 large red pepper

1 large yellow pepper

250 g dried orzo pasta

20 cherry tomatoes

400-g tin or jar artichoke hearts, drained and quartered

1 small red onion, thinly sliced

4 tablespoons fresh or bottled pesto

4 tablespoons pine nuts, toasted

a handful of basil leaves

sea salt and freshly ground black pepper

SERVES 4

This colourful salad can be made well ahead of time, just cook and add the lamb before serving. It's full of the flavours of summer.

Preheat the oven to 220°C (425°F) Gas 7 and the grill to hot.

Combine the garlic and lemon zest with 1 tablespoon of the oil in a small bowl and season with salt and pepper. Rub this over the lamb and set aside until needed.

Put the lamb under the hot grill and cook for 2 minutes each side, then transfer to a roasting tray and cook in the oven for 5 minutes for medium rare or up to 10 minutes for more well done. Remove from the oven, wrap in foil and leave to rest for 10 minutes.

Cut the peppers into thick strips, discarding the stems and seeds. Cook under the hot grill until tender. Set aside.

Bring a large saucepan of salted water to the boil. Add the orzo and cook until al dente, or according to the packet instructions. Drain and toss with the remaining oil, lemon juice, peppers, cherry tomatoes, artichokes, onion and pesto.

Place the salad on a serving platter. Slice the lamb and arrange it on top. Scatter with the pine nuts and basil leaves.

meat and poultry

penne with chilli meatballs

2 tablespoons olive oil

1 onion, chopped

2 garlic cloves, crushed

2 x 400-g tins chopped tomatoes

1 tablespoon tomato purée

½ teaspoon caster sugar

½ teaspoon dried chilli flakes

400 g skinless beef sausages or plain beef sausages

400 g dried penne, or other pasta tube of your choice

freshly grated Parmesan cheese, to serve

sea salt and freshly ground black pepper

SERVES 4

These hearty meatballs are ready in just 15 minutes, making them ideal for a speedy mid-week supper. The chilli flakes give them a delicious kick.

Heat the oil in a frying pan set over high heat. Add the onion and garlic and cook, stirring, for 2–3 minutes, until softened and starting to turn golden.

Add the tomatoes, tomato purée, sugar, chilli flakes and 125 ml water and bring to the boil. Reduce the heat to a simmer.

Using slightly wet hands, squeeze the filling out of the sausage casings, if necessary, and shape into walnut-sized balls. Add these to the tomato sauce. Simmer the meatballs in the sauce for 5 minutes, shaking the pan often to move the meatballs around so that they cook evenly.

Bring a large saucepan of salted water to the boil. Add the pasta and cook until al dente, or according to the packet instructions.

Drain the pasta well and return it to the warm pan. Season the meatball sauce to taste with salt and pepper. Divide the pasta between 4 serving plates or bowls and top with meatballs. Sprinkle with grated Parmesan, then serve.

classic bolognese

There are countless versions of bolognese sauce. Some Italian chefs add sweetbreads, chicken livers and veal, but this version contains a mixture of beef mince and Parma ham. It really benefits from being chilled overnight, so it's ideal for making the day before and gently reheating.

10 g dried porcini mushrooms, rinsed

1 tablespoon olive oil

1 onion, finely chopped

500 g beef mince

50 g Parma ham, coarsely chopped

100 ml Marsala or sherry

700 ml tomato passata

300 g dried pasta, such as spaghetti or linguine

sea salt and freshly ground black pepper

fresh shavings of Parmesan cheese, to serve

SERVES 4

Put the mushrooms in a bowl, add enough boiling water to cover, then soak for 20 minutes. Squeeze them dry and chop finely.

Heat the oil in a large saucepan, add the onion and cook for 2 minutes. Add the beef mince and Parma ham and cook for 3–4 minutes, stirring, until evenly browned.

Drain the porcini and discard the soaking water. Chop the porcini, then add to the pan with the Marsala and passata. Cover and simmer for 1 hour, stirring occasionally, until rich and dark. Add salt and pepper to taste.

Around 10 minutes before the sauce is ready, bring a large pan of salted water to the boil. Add the pasta and cook until al dente, or according to the packet instructions. Drain well.

Divide the pasta between 4 serving plates or bowls. Top with the bolognese sauce and Parmesan shavings, then serve.

This light meat sauce is swelled with tomatoes, mushrooms and pine nuts. It is a lot less rich than a typical bolognese sauce and lower in fat too.

ligurian meat sauce

10 g dried porcini mushrooms

3 tablespoons olive oil

1 onion, finely chopped

100 g lean minced beef

25 g pine nuts

400 g tinned tomatoes, drained
(reserve the juices), deseeded
and chopped

1 tablespoon finely chopped mixed
rosemary and thyme leaves,
plus 1 teaspoon of each to serve

500 g dried pasta, such as tagliatelle,
spaghettini or ridged penne

3 tablespoons freshly grated
Parmesan cheese, plus extra to serve

sea salt and freshly ground
black pepper

SERVES 4–6

Put the mushrooms in a bowl, add enough boiling water to cover, then soak for 20 minutes. Squeeze them dry and chop finely.

Heat the oil in a large saucepan, add the onion and cook over low heat until soft. Increase the heat, add the meat and fry until browned. Add the pine nuts, mushrooms, tomatoes, herbs and salt and pepper, stir well and cover with a lid. Reduce the heat and cook slowly for 1 hour. Stir at regular intervals and, if necessary, add a little of the reserved tomato juice to keep the sauce moist.

Around 10 minutes before the sauce is ready, bring a large pan of salted water to the boil. Add the pasta and cook until al dente, or according to the packet instructions. Drain well.

Add the sauce and Parmesan to the pasta and mix well. Serve at once, sprinkled with extra herbs. Serve the extra cheese separately.

Variation Use minced pork, veal or lean lamb instead of beef.

italian meatballs with tomato sauce and spaghetti

300–400 g dried spaghetti

sea salt and freshly ground black pepper

tomato sauce

4 tablespoons extra virgin olive oil

3 garlic cloves, thinly sliced

1 large onion, cut into wedges

2 x 400-g tins chopped tomatoes

20 g basil leaves, plus extra to serve

meatballs

250 g beef mince

100 g fresh white breadcrumbs

2 eggs

25 g freshly grated Parmesan cheese, plus extra to serve

4 tablespoons chopped parsley

3 tablespoons extra virgin olive oil

SERVES 4

A simple tomato sauce is all that's needed to go with these tasty meatballs. They taste great accompanied by a bottle of Chianti or another full-bodied red wine.

To make the tomato sauce, put the oil, garlic, onion, tomatoes and basil in a saucepan, season well and bring to the boil. Reduce the heat and simmer gently for at least 40 minutes while you prepare the meatballs.

Preheat the oven to 200°C (400°F) Gas 6.

Meanwhile, put the beef, breadcrumbs, eggs, Parmesan, parsley and oil in a large mixing bowl, season and combine with your hands. Shape the mixture into roughly 20 walnut-sized balls and put in a single layer on a baking sheet covered with foil. Roast for 10 minutes, turn, then roast for a further 6–7 minutes.

Bring a large pan of salted water to the boil. Add the pasta and cook until al dente, or according to the packet instructions. Drain well, return to the pan and add the tomato sauce and meatballs. Stir very gently so as not to break up the meatballs. Take out the onion wedges if you prefer. Divide between 4 serving plates or bowls and top with the basil leaves and grated Parmesan.

herby steak sauce

1 tablespoon chopped rosemary

2 tablespoons chopped flat leaf parsley, plus extra to serve

2 garlic cloves, crushed

4 sunblush tomatoes or sun-dried tomatoes

2 teaspoons salted capers, rinsed well

8 minute steaks, 50 g each

1 tablespoon olive oil

2 x 400-g tins plum tomatoes

300 g dried pasta, such as conchiglie or rigatoni

sea salt and freshly ground black pepper

SERVES 4

The combination of fresh herbs, sunblush tomatoes and capers makes this steak sauce an indulgent dish that is sure to delight the taste buds.

Put the rosemary, parsley, garlic, sunblush or sun-dried tomatoes and capers into a food processor and process until finely chopped.

Put the steaks flat onto a work surface and sprinkle lightly with salt and pepper. Spread the herb mixture evenly over each steak and roll up tightly, tying string around the middle to secure.

Heat the oil until very hot in a large frying pan, add the rolled steaks and cook for 2–3 minutes until browned all over. Add the tinned tomatoes and salt and pepper to taste. Cover and simmer for 1 hour, then remove the lid and cook for a further 20 minutes until the meat is tender and the sauce has thickened.

Bring a large pan of salted water to the boil. Add the pasta and cook until al dente, or according to the packet instructions.

Transfer the steaks from the sauce to a chopping board. Discard the string, then cut each steak crossways into chunky slices.

Drain the pasta and return it to the warm pan. Add the sauce and steak to the pasta and toss to mix. Divide between 4 serving bowls or plates, top with parsley and serve.

1 garlic clove, chopped

1 red chilli, deseeded and
finely chopped

4 sun-dried tomatoes in oil, drained
and coarsely chopped

500 g pork mince

1 teaspoon fresh thyme leaves

4 tablespoons freshly grated
Parmesan cheese, plus extra to serve

1 quantity Fresh Pasta Dough,
rolled (page 12) or 500 g fresh
lasagne sheets

1 quantity Tomato Sauce with Double
Basil (page 119), warmed

a handful of basil leaves, to serve

sea salt and freshly ground
black pepper

SERVES 4

pork and parmesan ravioli

Pork and cheese are not a common pairing, but they make a good match if full-bodied flavours such as garlic and sun-dried tomatoes are included in the mix. The filling can be made in advance and kept covered and refrigerated for up to a day.

Put the garlic, chilli and sun-dried tomatoes into a food processor and process until finely chopped. Add the pork, thyme, Parmesan, salt and pepper, then process again until evenly blended.

Put a sheet of rolled pasta onto a lightly floured surface. Put tablespoons of the mixture in evenly spaced mounds on the dough, leaving about 4 cm between each mound. Cover with a second sheet of rolled pasta dough and, using your fingers, press firmly round the mounds to seal, excluding any air.

Using a knife, cut lines between the mounds to make separate squares, about 8 cm each. Repeat with the remaining pasta and filling to make 20 ravioli squares in total.

Bring a large saucepan of water to the boil. Add a good pinch of salt, then the ravioli, and cook for 3–4 minutes until they rise to the surface and are cooked through. Drain carefully and return to the warm pan. Add the warm tomato sauce and stir to coat. Divide between 4 serving plates or bowls, sprinkle with the basil leaves, pepper and Parmesan, then serve.

pork and lemon ragu

2 tablespoons olive oil

400 g pork mince

1 onion, finely chopped

2 garlic cloves, thinly sliced

4 anchovy fillets in oil, drained

2 tablespoons rosemary leaves

finely grated zest and juice of
1 unwaxed lemon

375 g dried rigatoni

500 ml whole milk

75 g green olives, stoned
and chopped

75 ml double cream

a good grating of fresh nutmeg

4 tablespoons Parmesan shavings,
plus extra to serve

sea salt and freshly ground
black pepper

SERVES 4

In Italy, pork is often braised with milk, as it
tenderizes the meat and the juices mingle with the
milk to provide a sweet, meaty sauce. Rosemary
is lovely and robust with pork but you could use
chopped sage – just add it earlier when you brown
the pork so it crisps up a little bit.

Heat the oil in a large frying pan over high heat and add the pork.
Leave it for a few minutes until it browns, then turn it over to allow
the other side to brown. Add the onion, garlic, anchovies, rosemary
and lemon zest and stir to combine with the pork. Reduce the
heat, cover and leave the onion to soften for 10 minutes, stirring
occasionally so the ingredients don't stick to the bottom of the pan.

Bring a large pan of salted water to the boil. Add the pasta and
cook until al dente, or according to the packet instructions.

When the onion is translucent, add the milk, lemon juice and
olives, and bring to the boil, uncovered, scraping the base of the
pan to loosen any sticky, flavoursome bits and incorporating them
into the sauce. Simmer for about 15–20 minutes, or until about
two-thirds of the liquid has evaporated and the pork is soft.
Remove from the heat, stir in the cream, then season with salt,
pepper and nutmeg.

Drain the pasta, put it back in its pan and spoon in the pork ragu.
Add the Parmesan shavings, stir well and divide between 4 serving
plates or bowls. Sprinkle with the extra Parmesan shavings.

smoky chorizo and prawn gnocchetti

200 g large raw prawns, peeled and deveined

1 tablespoon red wine vinegar

2 tablespoons olive oil

1 red onion, chopped

1 green pepper, deseeded and thinly sliced

100 g chorizo sausage, finely chopped

½ teaspoon smoked paprika (pimentón)

400-g tin chopped tomatoes

300 g dried gnocchetti or any other pasta shape, such as fusilli or penne

1 tablespoon chopped mint leaves

1 tablespoon roughly chopped flat leaf parsley

sea salt and freshly ground black pepper

lemon wedges, to serve

SERVES 4

This is a lovely summery pasta dish, perfect for enjoying al fresco. Its influences are part-Italian and part-Spanish, which can mean only one thing: it's a sexy little number, perfect for effortless entertaining.

Put the prawns in a stainless steel or non-reactive bowl with the vinegar and 1 tablespoon of the oil. Season and set aside.

Heat the remaining oil in a heavy-based saucepan set over high heat. Add the onion, green pepper and chorizo and cook for 4–5 minutes, until softened and aromatic. Add the paprika and cook for 1 minute, stirring to combine. Add the tomatoes and 125 ml water and bring to the boil. Cook for 5 minutes, until the sauce has thickened slightly. Set aside while you cook the pasta.

Bring a large saucepan of salted water to the boil. Add the pasta and cook until al dente, or according to the instructions on the packet. Drain well and return to the warm pan. Add the tomato sauce and keep warm over very low heat while cooking the prawns.

Heat a non-stick frying pan over high heat. Cook the prawns for 2 minutes each side until pink.

Stir the prawns through the pasta and season to taste. Divide between 4 plates or bowls and scatter the mint and parsley over each one. Serve with lemon wedges on the side for squeezing.

aubergine and sausage rigatoni with red wine

This is a really robust pasta dish that's perfect to serve in cold weather. The wine gives a richer, more warming flavour than the usual tomato-based sauce.

350 g Italian sausages or other coarsely ground 100% pork sausages

4 tablespoons olive oil

1 medium aubergine, cut into cubes

1 medium onion, finely chopped

1 red pepper, deseeded and cut into 2-cm cubes

1 rounded tablespoon tomato purée

2 garlic cloves, crushed

1 teaspoon dried oregano

175 ml Zinfandel or other full-bodied, fruity red wine

175 ml fresh chicken stock or light vegetable stock made from 1 teaspoon vegetable bouillon powder

350 g dried pasta tubes, such as rigatoni or penne

4 tablespoons chopped parsley

sea salt and freshly ground black pepper

SERVES 4

Slit the sausage skins with a sharp knife, peel them off and discard. Roughly chop the sausage meat. Heat 1 tablespoon olive oil in a large frying pan, add the sausage meat, breaking it up with a spatula or wooden spoon, and fry until lightly golden. Using a slotted spoon, remove the meat from the pan and set aside.

Add 2 more tablespoons oil to the pan, add the aubergine and stir-fry for 3–4 minutes until it starts to brown. Add the remaining oil and the chopped onion and fry for 1–2 minutes. Add the red pepper and fry for another 1–2 minutes. Return the sausage meat to the pan, stir in the tomato purée and cook for 1 minute. Add the garlic, oregano and wine and simmer until the wine has reduced by half. Stir in the stock and let simmer over low heat for about 10 minutes.

Meanwhile, bring a large saucepan of salted water to the boil. Add the pasta and cook until al dente, or according to the instructions on the packet. When the pasta is just cooked, spoon off a couple of tablespoons of the cooking water and stir it into the wine sauce. Drain the pasta thoroughly, then tip it into the sauce. Add 3 tablespoons parsley and mix well. Remove the pan from the heat, cover and let stand for 2–3 minutes for the flavours to amalgamate.

Check the seasoning, adding salt and pepper to taste, then spoon the pasta and sauce into 4 warm serving plates or bowls. Serve immediately, sprinkled with the remaining parsley.

country sausage, peas and tomatoes

2 tablespoons olive oil

8 Italian-style sausages

200 ml stock, such as chicken, beef or vegetable

500 g dried pasta, such as ridged penne or tubetti

1 small onion, finely chopped

1 kg fresh peas, shelled, or 250 g frozen peas

1 teaspoon icing sugar

1 tablespoon chopped parsley

200 g cherry tomatoes, halved

3 tablespoons freshly grated Parmesan cheese, plus extra, to serve

SERVES 4–6

This version of a traditional country recipe uses Italian sausages rather than pancetta as its base. The contrast in flavour and texture of the meaty coarse sausage, the sweetness of the peas and colourful cherry tomatoes works very well.

Cover the base of a frying pan with the oil, then set over medium heat. Add the sausages and cook over low heat, turning until they are brown all over. Pour off the excess fat and reserve. Cut the sausages in half, scrape out the meat and discard the skins. Put the sausage meat back in the pan and add a little stock to deglaze. Simmer for a few minutes, stirring the resulting pan juices into the sausage meat. The whole process will take about 20–30 minutes.

Meanwhile, bring a large saucepan of salted water to the boil. Add the pasta and cook until al dente, or according to the instructions on the packet. Drain well and set aside.

Pour a little of the reserved sausage fat into a clean frying pan and heat through. Add the onion and cook over gentle heat until soft. Add the peas, icing sugar, parsley and enough stock to cover the ingredients. Cover with a lid and cook until the peas are tender. If you are using frozen peas, add them with the onions and 100 ml stock then heat through.

Stir the peas into the sausage meat and let simmer for 5 minutes. When ready to serve, increase the heat, add the tomatoes and cook quickly until the edges start to wilt. Add the sauce to the pasta, stir in the Parmesan and mix well. Serve with extra cheese.

Variation Instead of the peas, stir in cooked fagioli or other beans after cooking the onion. Add a few chopped tomatoes and cook for 10–15 minutes or until the tomatoes are thick and creamy. Proceed as in the main recipe.

sausage ragu

750 g fresh spicy chorizo sausage

2 tablespoons extra virgin olive oil

1 onion, finely chopped

2 garlic cloves, crushed

2 tablespoons chopped sage

2 x 400-g tins chopped tomatoes

125 ml red wine

2 tablespoons tomato purée

2 tablespoons chopped
flat leaf parsley

500 g dried pasta

sea salt and freshly ground
black pepper

SERVES 4–6

This rich chorizo ragu is great for making ahead of time. In fact, it tastes better served the next day when the ingredients have had a chance to mingle.

Split open the sausage skins, peel them off and discard. Roughly chop the sausage meat, put in a food processor and pulse until it is coarsely ground.

Heat the oil in a saucepan and gently fry the onion, garlic, sage and seasoning over low heat for 10 minutes, or until soft and lightly golden. Add the sausage meat and stir-fry over medium heat for 5 minutes, or until browned.

Add the tomatoes, wine and tomato purée, bring to the boil, cover and simmer gently for 1 hour, or until the sauce has thickened. Season to taste and stir in the parsley.

Towards the end of the cooking time for the sauce, bring a large saucepan of salted water to the boil. Add the pasta and cook until al dente, or according to the instructions on the packet. Drain well and divide between 4–6 serving plates or bowls, top with the ragu and serve immediately.

ham and pea fusilli

300 g dried fusilli

1 tablespoon olive oil

1 shallot, diced

1 garlic clove, crushed

200 g cooked ham, chopped

200 g peas, fresh or frozen
(no need to thaw)

100 ml double cream

2 egg yolks

75 g Parmesan cheese, grated

sea salt and freshly ground
black pepper

SERVES 4

This creamy dish is far richer in flavour than the short list of ingredients would have you believe. Not only that but it takes just 15 minutes to cook.

Bring a large saucepan of salted water to the boil. Add the pasta and cook until al dente, or according to the instructions on the packet. Drain well and set aside.

Meanwhile, heat the oil in a saucepan, add the shallot and garlic and fry over a low heat until soft.

Put the ham, peas and cream in another pan and heat to a gentle simmer. Take off the heat and add the egg yolks, Parmesan and seasoning. Mix well so that the egg does not scramble. Finally, add the fried garlic and shallot, toss through the pasta and serve.

ham and mushroom mezzalune

Truffle oil's earthy flavour goes beautifully with mushrooms and makes a great finishing touch to these mezzalune. If you don't have any, use olive oil. To make the soft Taleggio easier to slice thinly, put it in the freezer for 10–15 minutes beforehand.

2 tablespoons olive oil

1 garlic clove, finely chopped

250 g small chestnut or field mushrooms, sliced

2 tablespoons Marsala or medium sherry

1 quantity Fresh Pasta, rolled into 4 sheets (page 12) or 500g fresh lasagne sheets

200 g Taleggio cheese, thinly cut into 12 slices

6 slices Parma ham, halved

sea salt and freshly ground black pepper

truffle oil or olive oil, to serve

basil leaves, to serve

SERVES 4

Heat the oil in a frying pan, add the garlic and cook for 1 minute. Add the mushrooms and seasoning to taste and cook for 3–4 minutes until golden. Add the Marsala, remove from the heat and leave to cool.

Put a rolled pasta sheet onto a lightly floured surface. Put the bowl, upside down, on top of the pasta and cut round it with a knife. Repeat to make 12 rounds from the 4 pasta sheets. Put a slice of Taleggio on one side of each round, add a spoonful of mushrooms and top with a piece of Parma ham, folded to fit if necessary. Dampen the edges lightly with water and fold each circle over to form a semicircle, pressing the edges together firmly to enclose the filling and seal.

Bring a large saucepan of water to the boil. Add a good pinch of salt, then half the mezzalune. Cook for 3–4 minutes until they rise to the surface and are cooked through. Drain carefully and keep them warm while you cook the remaining mezzalune. Divide between 4 plates, sprinkle with truffle or olive oil, basil leaves and black pepper, then serve.

Note If you are not cooking the mezzalune immediately, arrange them in a single layer on a tray lined with greaseproof paper, cover with another sheet of greaseproof paper and keep in the refrigerator for up to 2 hours.

300 g peas, fresh or frozen and defrosted

4 tablespoons extra virgin olive oil

5 tablespoons fresh breadcrumbs

500 g dried linguine

90 g thinly sliced pancetta, chopped

3 garlic cloves, crushed

a few sprigs of sage, leaves finely chopped

5 tablespoons dry white wine

25 g freshly grated Parmesan cheese

1 tablespoon chopped flat leaf parsley

sea salt and freshly ground black pepper

SERVES 4–6

linguine with peas, pancetta and sage

This makes a great midweek supper dish but is smart enough to entertain with too. It also makes an interesting change from tomato-based sauces.

Lightly blanch the peas in a saucepan of boiling water for 2–3 minutes. Drain and set aside.

Heat 2 tablespoons of the oil in a frying pan. Add the breadcrumbs and cook until toasted, stirring occasionally, about 3 minutes. Season lightly and set aside.

Bring a large saucepan of salted water to the boil. Add the pasta and cook until al dente, or according to the instructions on the packet. Drain well and set aside.

Heat 1 tablespoon oil in a saucepan large enough to hold all the pasta later. Add the pancetta and cook, stirring, until browned, about 2 minutes. Add the garlic and cook, stirring, for 1 minute. Stir in the sage leaves and wine. Cook, stirring, until the liquid has almost evaporated, about 1 minute.

Add the drained pasta to the pan of pancetta. Then add the peas and the remaining oil and cook over low heat, tossing well to mix. Stir in the Parmesan, parsley and pepper; taste and add salt and more pepper if necessary. Sprinkle with the toasted breadcrumbs and serve immediately.

amatriciana

2 tablespoons olive oil

200 g pancetta or streaky bacon, cut into thin strips

a piece of dried chilli, to taste

1 onion, finely chopped

800 g tinned tomatoes, drained (retain the juice), deseeded and chopped

500 g dried pasta, such as bucatini, spaghetti or penne

1 tablespoon chopped parsley

3 tablespoons freshly grated pecorino or Parmesan cheese, plus extra, to serve

sea salt and freshly ground black pepper

extra virgin olive oil, to serve

SERVES 4–6

This well-known recipe is synonymous with the robust traditional cooking of Rome. The sauce is made with fried pancetta and onions, flavoured with chilli and cooked in tomato. Traditionally it is served with bucatini, thick spaghetti-like pasta with a hole running though the middle.

Heat the oil in a frying pan, add the pancetta and chilli and cook until the pancetta fat runs. Then add the onion and fry over low heat until transparent.

Add the tomatoes, cover and cook over low heat for 30 minutes. Stir often to prevent sticking, adding a little of the tomato juice to the pan if necessary. Discard the chilli and season to taste. At this stage the sauce can be rested and reheated when required.

Towards the end of the cooking time for the sauce, bring a large saucepan of salted water to the boil. Add the pasta and cook until al dente, or according to the instructions on the packet.

Drain the pasta thoroughly and stir in the sauce. Mix in the parsley along with 3 tablespoons cheese. Serve at once, sprinkled with extra cheese and drizzled with extra virgin olive oil.

pancetta and bean rigatoni

1 tablespoon olive oil

1 onion, chopped

1 garlic clove, finely chopped

1 teaspoon dried oregano

140 g pancetta or lean smoky bacon, roughly chopped

400 ml passata

a pinch of sugar

1 teaspoon tomato purée

100 g tinned borlotti beans, drained and rinsed

200 g dried rigatoni

sea salt and freshly ground black pepper

SERVES 2

Rustic and hearty, this pasta dish makes for a warming supper. Tinned beans are a convenient store-cupboard standby, and as well as providing slow-release energy and low-fat protein, three heaped tablespoons count as a single portion of the recommended 'five-a-day'.

Heat the oil in a saucepan and fry the onion gently for around 8 minutes until softened, then stir in the garlic, oregano and pancetta and cook for another 2 minutes.

Pour in the passata and stir in the sugar and tomato purée. Bring to the boil, then reduce the heat to low and simmer, half-covered, for 10 minutes, stirring occasionally. Add the beans, stir and cook for another 5 minutes.

Bring a large saucepan of salted water to the boil. Add the pasta and cook until al dente, or according to the instructions on the packet. Drain, reserving 4 tablespoons of the cooking water.

Add the cooked pasta and reserved cooking water to the sauce and heat through before serving. Season to taste.

pancetta and chicken meatballs

500 g chicken mince

50 g thinly sliced pancetta, coarsely chopped

6 spring onions, finely chopped

4 garlic cloves, finely chopped

2 red chillies, deseeded and finely chopped

4 tablespoons freshly grated Parmesan cheese, plus extra to serve

1 tablespoon thyme leaves

1 tablespoon olive oil

200 ml red wine

2 x 400-g tins plum tomatoes

a pinch of sugar

300 g dried pasta, such as gnocchi or conchiglie

sea salt and freshly ground black pepper

SERVES 4

Meatballs are a time-honoured accompaniment to pasta. These delicious little mouthfuls are made with chicken, bacon and herbs, so are somewhat lighter than the traditional all-meat versions.

Put the mince, pancetta, spring onions, garlic, chillies, Parmesan and thyme into a bowl. Add plenty of salt and pepper and mix well. Using your hands, shape into 24 small, firm balls.

Heat the oil in a large saucepan, add the meatballs and cook for about 5 minutes, turning them frequently until browned all over. Add the wine and simmer vigorously for 1–2 minutes.

Add the tomatoes, breaking them up with a wooden spoon. Stir in the sugar, and add salt and pepper to taste. Bring to the boil, then simmer very gently, uncovered, for 30 minutes until the sauce is rich and thickened.

Meanwhile, bring a large saucepan of salted water to the boil. Add the pasta and cook until al dente, or according to the instructions on the packet.

Drain the pasta well and return it to the warm pan. Add the meatballs and sauce to the pasta, toss well to mix, then divide between 4 bowls. Serve topped with extra Parmesan.

This really is a great dish – tarragon and chicken go together so well. Pesto can be made from most herbs, so don't hesitate to try your own version in this recipe using one or more herb varieties.

300 g dried penne

9 tablespoons olive oil

75 g freshly grated Parmesan cheese

75 g pan-toasted pine nuts

2 tablespoons chopped tarragon

grated zest and freshly squeezed juice of 1 unwaxed lemon

1 garlic clove, thinly chopped

3 cooked chicken breasts, sliced

100 g rocket

sea salt and freshly ground black pepper

SERVES 4

chicken and tarragon pesto pasta

Bring a large saucepan of salted water to the boil. Add the pasta and cook until al dente, or according to the instructions on the packet. Drain and refresh the pasta in cold water, then drain thoroughly and toss in 4 tablespoons of the oil.

To make the pesto, put the Parmesan, pine nuts, tarragon, lemon zest and juice, garlic and remaining oil in a jug and purée until smooth with a hand-held blender.

Put the pasta, pesto, chicken and rocket in a serving bowl, season and toss well, coating the pasta and chicken evenly with the pesto.

Variation Replace the chicken with steamed vegetables such as courgettes, sugarsnap peas, broad beans or runner beans for a meatfree dish packed with a variety of vitamins.

Here are all the flavours and crunch of chicken Kiev. Of course, making your own is not only much tastier, but with thick strands of pappardelle to soak up the buttery juices, it's good bowl food, too. Turkey escalopes or cod fillets work just as well.

pappardelle with breaded chicken and garlic-parsley butter

1 egg, beaten

75 g fresh white breadcrumbs

3 skinless chicken breasts

4 tablespoons plain flour

300 g dried pappardelle

3–4 tablespoons extra virgin olive oil

75 g butter

2 garlic cloves, crushed

1 tablespoon chopped flat leaf parsley

25 g Parmesan cheese shavings

sea salt and freshly ground black pepper

SERVES 4

Prepare one bowl with the beaten egg and another with the breadcrumbs. Put one chicken breast in a freezer bag and bash with a rolling pin until flattened out. Spoon some of the flour into the bag, season well and shake until the chicken is coated. Dip the chicken in the egg, then in the breadcrumbs and set aside. Repeat the entire process with the remaining chicken breasts.

Bring a large saucepan of salted water to the boil. Add the pasta and cook until al dente, or according to the packet instructions.

Meanwhile, heat the oil in a large frying pan over medium heat and add the chicken in a single layer. Cook for 2–3 minutes, then turn over and cook the other side for the same amount of time, or until both sides are golden.

Lift the chicken onto a chopping board. Add the butter to the pan along with the garlic and parsley and leave to cook over low heat until the garlic and butter are about to colour. Season generously. Cut the chicken into strips and return to the pan.

Drain the pasta (reserving a cup of the water), slide it all back into the pan you cooked it in and tip in the chicken with all its juices. Give it a good stir, add the reserved water to keep the pasta moist and transfer to bowls. Sprinkle with Parmesan shavings.

fish and seafood

monkfish and italian vegetables with olives and capers

500 g monkfish tail

4 tablespoons olive oil

2 shallots, finely chopped

300 g baby courgettes cut into bite-sized pieces

300 g red peppers, halved, deseeded and cut into bite-sized pieces

125 ml white wine

2½ tablespoons capers

500 g dried pasta, such as farfalle or tagliatelle

250 g tomatoes, skinned, deseeded and chopped

1½ tablespoons pitted black olives

sea salt and freshly ground black pepper

25 basil leaves or 1 tablespoon chopped parsley, to serve

extra virgin olive oil, to serve

SERVES 4–6

The combination of monkfish, Mediterranean vegetables, capers and olives makes for a mouth-watering meal that is full of the flavours of summer.

Wipe the fish and cut into 4 equal pieces, discarding any bones. Season, arrange in an oiled roasting tin and set aside.

Preheat the oven to 200°C (400°F) Gas 6.

Heat 2 tablespoons of the olive oil in a frying pan, then add the shallots. Cook until soft, then raise the heat, add the courgettes and peppers and brown quickly. Add the wine, and when it has evaporated, add the capers, stir well, then season to taste.

Meanwhile, bring a large saucepan of salted water to the boil. Add the pasta and cook until al dente, or according to the instructions on the packet.

Spoon the cooked vegetables over the fish in the roasting tin until covered. Add the chopped tomatoes, olives and remaining olive oil. Cover the tin with foil and cook in the preheated oven for 8 minutes. Remove from the oven, discard the foil, cut the fish into bite-sized pieces and mix carefully into the vegetables.

Add the fish and vegetables and their cooking juices to the drained pasta and mix well, then stir in the basil or parsley and oil.

Variations Try thick cod, halibut, salmon or haddock fillets rather than monkfish tails. Use leeks, fennel bulbs, mushrooms and aubergines instead of peppers and courgettes.

'Tartare' means uncooked so this recipe calls for very fresh, sashimi-grade tuna. If you prefer your tuna cooked, sear it on a preheated stove-top grill pan for 1 minute on each side or until cooked to your liking.

chilli tuna tartare pasta

350 g dried fusilli or other pasta

6 tablespoons extra virgin olive oil, plus extra for serving

4 garlic cloves, sliced

1–2 dried red chillies, deseeded and chopped

grated zest and freshly squeezed juice of 1 unwaxed lemon

1 tablespoon chopped thyme leaves

500 g tuna steak, cut into chunks

a handful of basil leaves

sea salt and freshly ground black pepper

SERVES 4

Bring a large saucepan of salted water to the boil. Add the pasta and cook until al dente, or according to the instructions on the packet. Drain well and set aside.

Meanwhile, heat the oil in a frying pan, add the garlic and fry gently for 2 minutes until lightly golden. Add the chilli, lemon zest and thyme and fry for another minute.

Drain the pasta, reserving 4 tablespoons of the cooking liquid, and return both to the pan. Stir in the hot garlic oil mixture, lemon juice, tuna, basil leaves, salt and pepper and a little extra olive oil. Serve at once.

creamy smoked salmon sauce

300 g dried pasta, such as fusilli bucati or farfalle

300 ml double cream

2 garlic cloves, crushed

200 g smoked salmon, cut into 1-cm strips

4 tablespoons freshly grated Parmesan cheese, plus extra to serve

sea salt and freshly ground black pepper

2 tablespoons snipped chives, to serve

SERVES 4

Smoked salmon adds a lovely delicate flavour to this dish. Add it right at the last moment so that it doesn't overcook or break into tiny pieces.

Bring a large saucepan of salted water to the boil. Add the pasta and cook until al dente, or according to the packet instructions.

Meanwhile, put the cream and garlic into a small saucepan. Add salt and pepper to taste and heat gently until warmed through.

Drain the pasta and return it to the warm pan. Add the cream, smoked salmon and Parmesan, toss gently, then divide between 4 serving bowls or plates. Sprinkle with chives and extra Parmesan cheese and serve.

The combination of cream, fish and basil always makes for a wonderfully delicious dish. Remember to provide finger bowls for your guests as the prawns are served with their shells left on.

prawns and salmon with a citrus cream sauce

300 g dried egg pasta, such as pappardelle or tagliatelle

100 g peeled prawns, plus 150 g small cooked prawn tails, shells on, such as Icelandic prawns

200 ml single cream

50 g unsalted butter

200 g thick salmon fillet, cut into thin slices across the grain of the fish

olive oil, to taste

finely chopped zest of 1 lemon and freshly squeezed juice of ½ a lemon

20 basil leaves, thinly sliced

sea salt and freshly ground black pepper

SERVES 4

Bring a large saucepan of salted water to the boil. Add the pasta and cook until al dente, or according to the packet instructions.

Meanwhile, put the peeled prawns in a food processor and blend to a paste. Put the cream, butter and pepper in a small saucepan and heat gently, shaking the pan from time to time. When the sauce has thickened, add the prawn paste to the cream, stir, cover and switch off the heat.

Preheat a stove-top grill pan until very hot. Arrange the strips of salmon across the ridges of the pan and cook quickly on both sides. Transfer the pieces to a plate as they brown, sprinkle with oil, lemon juice, salt and pepper.

Pan-grill the unshelled prawns, in batches if necessary, until aromatic and opaque. Do not overcook or they will be tough and tasteless. Set aside 8–12 prawns and 4 slices of the salmon for serving.

Add the sauce, prawns, salmon pieces and basil to the drained pasta and mix well. Divide between 4 serving plates or bowls. Make small piles of the reserved prawns and salmon on the top of each portion and sprinkle with lemon zest. Serve at once.

spaghetti and prawns with pesto, cooked in a paper bag

500 g dried spaghetti or similar

150 ml bought or fresh pesto sauce

1 garlic clove, crushed

750 g medium uncooked prawn tails, shells on

125 ml dry white wine

freshly ground black pepper

olive oil, for brushing

SERVES 4

This novel way of cooking pasta seals in all the delicious seafood juices and releases a wonderful aroma when each parcel is opened.

Preheat the oven to 200°C (400°F) Gas 6.

Cook the pasta in plenty of boiling salted water for 2 minutes only, then drain and mix with half the pesto.

Cut 4 x 30-cm squares of greaseproof paper and brush 1 teaspoon oil over the centre of each. Pile equal amounts of pasta in the middle of each square. Put the remaining pesto in a bowl, add the garlic and prawns and toss well. Divide between the squares. Season with black pepper and sprinkle each serving with 2 tablespoons wine.

Brush the edges of each paper square lightly with water, then bring up the paper loosely around the filling, twisting tightly to enclose. (The parcels should look like gathered money bags.) Put the parcels on a baking tray.

Bake in the preheated oven at or 10–15 minutes. Serve immediately, letting guests open their own parcels.

herbed tagliatelle with prawn skewers

350 g dried pasta, such as tagliatelle, linguine or fettuccine

20 uncooked tiger prawns, peeled with tails on

2 garlic cloves, crushed

½ teaspoon crushed dried chillies

4 tablespoons olive oil

1 teaspoon chopped rosemary

2 tablespoons chopped flat leaf parsley

1 tablespoon snipped chives

a handful of rocket

sea salt and freshly ground black pepper

1 lemon, cut into wedges, to serve

4 wooden skewers, soaked in water for 30 minutes

SERVES 4

A lovely, summery dish to make the most of fragrant garden herbs. Having the prawns on skewers adds a sense of occasion (and makes them easier to turn while cooking), but you can always cook them loose and add to the pasta just before serving.

Bring a large saucepan of salted water to the boil. Add the pasta and cook until al dente, or according to the packet instructions.

Preheat a stove-top grill pan until hot.

Meanwhile, put the prawns in a bowl and add the garlic, dried chillies, 1 tablespoon of the oil, and salt and pepper to taste. Mix well, then thread 5 prawns onto each skewer.

Add the prawn skewers to the hot grill pan and cook for 3 minutes on each side until pink and cooked through. Remove and keep them warm. Add the lemon wedges to the pan and cook quickly for 30 seconds on each side.

Drain the pasta and return it to the warm pan. Add the remaining oil, rosemary, parsley, chives and rocket, with salt and pepper to taste. Toss gently, then divide between 4 serving bowls. Top each with a prawn skewer and a lemon wedge for squeezing, then serve.

linguine with prawns, peas and lemon

200 g dried linguine

2 courgettes, sliced

100 g frozen petits pois

1 tablespoon olive oil

1 large garlic clove, finely chopped
(optional)

200 g cooked, shelled, deveined
large prawns

grated zest and 2 tablespoons freshly
squeezed juice of ½ unwaxed lemon

2 tablespoons crème fraîche

sea salt and freshly ground
black pepper

fresh basil leaves, to garnish

SERVES 2

This easy and revitalizing pasta dish is packed with
protein, zinc, folic acid and other B vitamins. It's
ready to serve in just 10 minutes.

Bring a large saucepan of salted water to the boil. Add the pasta
and cook until al dente, or according to the instructions on the
packet. Drain well, reserving 4 tablespoons of the cooking water.

Meanwhile, steam the courgettes and petits pois until cooked.

While the pasta and vegetables are cooking, heat the oil in
a heavy-based saucepan and fry the garlic, if using, over medium-
low heat for 1 minute. Add the prawns, lemon zest and juice,
crème fraîche and reserved cooking water. Cook, stirring, for
about 1 minute until the prawns are heated through.

Add the pasta, courgettes and petits pois and toss until the
ingredients are combined and warmed through. Season to taste
and serve sprinkled with basil leaves.

crab tortellini

2 tablespoons olive oil

1 shallot, finely chopped

2 garlic cloves, finely chopped

1 red chilli, deseeded and finely chopped

1 tablespoon chopped tarragon, plus extra leaves to serve

grated zest and juice of 1 unwaxed lemon

250 g fresh or tinned white crabmeat, drained if tinned

1 quantity Fresh Pasta Dough (see page 12)

50 g unsalted butter, cubed

sea salt and freshly ground black pepper

a plain pastry cutter, 5 cm diameter

SERVES 4

Make these very small shapes in batches, rolling out one sheet of dough at a time, so that the pasta doesn't dry out as you are working.

Heat the oil in a small frying pan, add the shallot, garlic and chilli and cook for 4–5 minutes until softened and golden. Remove from the heat and stir in the tarragon, half the lemon zest, the crabmeat, salt and pepper.

Divide the pasta dough into 6 and roll out 1 piece (see page 12). Put the sheet of rolled dough onto a lightly floured surface and, using the pastry cutter, stamp out 10–12 rounds. Put a small teaspoon of the mixture in the centre of each circle, brush water lightly round the edge of the circle and fold over to enclose the filling. Seal, excluding as much air as possible. Bring the two tips together and pinch firmly to seal them. Working in batches, repeat with the remaining pasta dough and filling mixture.

Bring a large saucepan of salted water to the boil. Add the tortellini and cook for 3–4 minutes until they rise to the surface and are cooked through.

Meanwhile, put the remaining lemon zest and juice into a small saucepan over low heat. Add the butter, 1 or 2 cubes at a time, stirring with a whisk until smooth and foaming. Carefully drain the tortellini, return them to the warm pan and add the lemon butter. Stir briefly, then divide between 4 bowls or plates. Top with a few tarragon leaves and plenty of pepper, then serve.

Note If you are not cooking the tortellini immediately, arrange in a single layer on a tray lined with greaseproof paper, cover with another sheet of greaseproof paper and chill for up to 2 hours.

linguine with garlic and chilli clams

1 kg fresh clams, well scrubbed

400 g dried linguine or spaghetti

65 ml extra virgin olive oil

3 garlic cloves, roughly chopped

2 large red chillies, deseeded and chopped

65 ml dry white wine

1 tablespoon roughly chopped flat leaf parsley

sea salt and freshly ground black pepper

crusty bread, to serve

SERVES 4

You will always see this dish on the menu at restaurants in Italy, especially in the coastal towns where good seafood is fresh, plentiful and cheap. It is one of those restaurant meals you can successfully cook at home in a flash. As always with dishes that have very few ingredients, the quality and freshness of those ingredients is key. Buy your clams as fresh as possible and try to find small ones.

Tap each clam lightly and discard any that won't close.

Bring a large saucepan of salted water to the boil. Add the pasta and cook until al dente, or according to the instructions on the packet. Drain well and set aside.

Meanwhile, heat the oil in a large saucepan set over medium heat. Add the garlic and chillies and cook until the garlic just starts to sizzle, flavouring the oil without burning. Increase the heat to high, add the wine and cook until it boils and has reduced by half.

Add the clams, cover the pan tightly and cook for 3–4 minutes, shaking the pan to encourage the clams to open. Discard any clams that don't open.

Add the pasta to the pan, toss to combine and season to taste with salt and pepper. Stir in the parsley and serve immediately with good crusty bread on the side for mopping up the juices.

pasta vongole

2 tablespoons olive oil

2 garlic cloves, finely chopped

a sprig of rosemary

500 ml tomato passata

½ teaspoon sugar

300 g dried pasta, such as spaghetti or linguine

1 kg fresh baby clams or cockles in shells

2 tablespoons chopped flat leaf parsley

sea salt and freshly ground black pepper

SERVES 4

The clams are the stars of this dish, but it's crucial that the sauce is smooth. If you have only tinned tomatoes, purée them with a hand-blender or press them through a sieve before using. Delicious as this is, it's not an elegant meal to eat, so be prepared: tie your napkin firmly round your neck and use your fingers to pick the clams from their shells.

Heat the oil in a saucepan, add the garlic and rosemary and cook for 2 minutes. Add the passata and sugar, with salt and pepper to taste. Bring to the boil, cover and simmer for 30 minutes, then remove and discard the sprig of rosemary.

Bring a large saucepan of salted water to the boil. Add the pasta and cook until al dente, or according to the packet instructions.

While the pasta is cooking, put the clams and 2 tablespoons water into another large saucepan. Cover and cook over medium heat for 4–5 minutes, shaking the pan occasionally until all the shells have opened, and discarding any that remain closed.

Strain the clam cooking juices through a sieve into the tomato pan, to remove grit. When the clams are cool enough to handle, shell half of them and discard the empty shells. Add the shelled and unshelled clams to the tomato sauce and simmer for 3–4 minutes.

Drain the pasta and return it to the warm pan. Add the clams and parsley and toss to mix. Divide between 4 serving plates or bowls and serve immediately.

mussels in white wine with linguine

300 g dried linguine or tagliatelle

150 ml dry white wine

2 garlic cloves, finely chopped

1 red chilli, deseeded and finely chopped

1 kg fresh mussels in shells, debearded and scrubbed

2 tablespoons chopped flat leaf parsley

sea salt and freshly ground black pepper

olive oil, to serve

SERVES 4

This is a delicious, low-fat pasta dish made with just a handful of ingredients. Better still, it's ready to serve in the time it takes to cook the linguine.

Bring a large saucepan of salted water to the boil. Add the pasta and cook until al dente, or according to the packet instructions.

Meanwhile, put the wine, garlic and chilli in a large saucepan, bring to the boil and simmer rapidly for 5 minutes. Add the mussels, cover with a lid and cook for a further 5 minutes, shaking the pan from time to time until all the shells have opened. Discard any that remain closed.

Add the parsley and mussels to the drained pasta and toss gently to mix. Add salt and pepper to taste. Divide between 4 serving plates or bowls, sprinkle with olive oil, then serve.

spaghetti with mussels, prawns, lemon and garlic

1 kg fresh mussels or clams, in their shells

125 ml white wine

1 shallot, finely chopped

400 g dried spaghetti or linguine

7 tablespoons extra virgin olive oil, plus extra to serve

¼ teaspoon dried red chilli flakes

1 garlic clove, finely chopped

350–400 g large uncooked prawns, peeled and deveined, tails left on

grated zest and 1 tablespoon freshly squeezed juice, plus extra to taste of ½ unwaxed lemon

3 tablespoons finely chopped flat leaf parsley

sea salt and freshly ground black pepper

SERVES 4

Seafood has its own sweetness that is always delicious with the sharpness of lemon. Together with gently cooked garlic and fiery red chilli, this makes a classic sauce to toss through cooked pasta – use a thin pasta, such as spaghetti or linguine. There is no need to serve Parmesan with this dish.

Scrub the mussels thoroughly and discard any that still gape open after cleaning. Put the wine and shallot in a large saucepan, bring to the boil and simmer for a few minutes. Add the mussels, cover tightly and cook over high heat for 4–5 minutes, shaking the pan 2 or 3 times, until all the mussels have opened. Drain, retaining the liquid and discard any mussels that haven't opened. Shell the mussels, retaining a few in the shell for serving.

Bring a large saucepan of salted water to the boil. Add the pasta and cook until al dente, or according to the packet instructions.

Meanwhile, put the oil in a wide pan over very low heat and let warm. Add the chilli flakes and cook very gently for 2–3 minutes before adding the garlic. Keep the heat very low – the garlic should barely bubble and certainly not brown – and shake the pan from time to time. Allow about 5 minutes for the flavours to infuse the oil. Add the prawns and cook gently until they turn pink and opaque, then put them on a plate. Add the mussel cooking liquid, lemon zest and lemon juice to the pan and cook quickly to reduce by a few spoonfuls. Add the cooked mussels and prawns to heat through.

When the pasta is ready, drain, then toss it immediately with the seafood and parsley, adding a little extra lemon juice to taste. Divide between 4 serving plates or bowls, season with pepper and serve immediately with extra virgin olive oil drizzled on top.

fishmarket sauce

This is the perfect sauce for a lavish occasion. The rich tomato concassé infused with saffron provides a perfect base for fresh seafood.

3 tablespoons extra virgin olive oil, plus extra to drizzle

2 garlic cloves, peeled and chopped

1 tablespoon chopped thyme

625 g ripe tomatoes, skinned and finely chopped

150 ml dry white wine

150 ml fish stock

a small pinch of saffron threads

400g dried spaghetti or linguine

2 x 350-g uncooked lobster tails

12 fresh mussels

12 large fresh scallops

12 large uncooked tiger prawns, shelled and deveined

2 tablespoons chopped basil

sea salt and freshly ground black pepper

SERVES 4

Heat the oil in a large, wide saucepan and gently fry the garlic and thyme for 3–4 minutes, or until soft but not browned. Add the tomatoes, stir well, then pour in the wine. Bring to the boil and simmer for 1 minute, then add the stock, saffron and seasoning. Cover and simmer over low heat for 30 minutes.

Bring a large saucepan of salted water to the boil. Add the pasta and cook until al dente, or according to the packet instructions.

Meanwhile, prepare the shellfish. Cut the lobster tails lengthways down the centre of the back and discard any intestinal tract, then cut, through the shell, into 4–5 pieces. (You can leave the shell on or take it off before cooking – if you leave it on, be sure to warn guests to watch out for the shell in the sauce.) Wash the mussels in several changes of cold water, scrub the shells clean and pull out the straggly 'beard' if still attached. Cut away the tough grey muscle at the side of each scallop.

Add the lobster and mussels to the tomato sauce and cook for 5 minutes, or until the mussels have opened. Discard any that remain closed. Add the prawns and cook for 2 minutes more, then add the scallops and cook for a further minute. Remove the pan from the heat and stir in the basil. Add the sauce to the drained pasta. Divide between 4 serving plates or bowls, sprinkle with olive oil and serve immediately.

pappardelle with seafood sauce

200 g Italian '00' flour or plain
white flour and extra flour or semolina
flour, for shaping

2 medium eggs

2 teaspoons sea salt flakes, crushed

180 ml extra virgin olive oil

450 g lobster meat, from 1 kg
whole lobster

bunch dill, chopped, about 40 g

bunch of chives, chopped,
about 40 g

grated zest and freshly squeezed
juice of 1 unwaxed lemon

sea salt and freshly crushed
black pepper

SERVES 4

Pappardelle is easier to make than most pastas
because you simply cut it into strips with a knife.

Put the flour, eggs and sea salt flakes into a food processor. Work
in bursts for about 1 minute until the mixture comes together in a
crumbly mass, then into a rough ball. Knead it firmly together and
remove to a floured work surface.

Knead by hand for 2 minutes, then wrap in clingfilm and chill
for 1 hour. Divide the dough into 4 parts, keeping 3 still wrapped.
Starting on the thickest setting of the pasta machine, roll 1 piece of
dough through, 3–4 times, folding the 2 ends into the middle each
time to get a plump envelope of dough and giving it a half turn
each time. Lightly flour the dough on both sides.

Roll it through all the settings on the pasta machine, starting at the
thickest, about 6 times in all, until you get a 1-metre length of pasta
(cut it in half if it's easier). Hang this over a chair or pole to air-dry.
Continue the process until all the pasta sheets are lined up. Roll
up each length, then slice into 2.5 cm wide ribbons (pappardelle).
Unroll, dust in semolina flour, then cut each in half, to make strips
about 50 cm long. Fill a large saucepan with hot water, add a pinch
of salt and bring to the boil.

Meanwhile, to make the sauce, warm the oil in a heavy-based
frying pan. Add the lobster meat, dill, chives, 1 tablespoon of the
lemon juice, salt and pepper. Heat briefly until the flavours blend
well. Leave on a very low heat to keep warm.

Add the pasta to the boiling salted water, cook for 1½ minutes,
then drain. Tip the pasta into the sauce, toss gently with 2 wooden
spoons, add the lemon zest and serve in pasta bowls.

Variation Use 500g fresh egg pappardelle instead of making
your own and cook according to the instructions above.

vegetables and herbs

pasta with fresh tomato

1 kg ripe tomatoes

6 tablespoons extra virgin olive oil

2 red chillies, deseeded and chopped

2 garlic cloves, crushed

1 tablespoon chopped basil

1 teaspoon sugar

350 g dried spaghetti

sea salt and freshly ground black pepper

grated pecorino or Parmesan cheese, to serve

SERVES 4

This sauce is best made as soon as the new season's tomatoes arrive in the shops, especially the vine-ripened varieties. If you don't have a gas hob, simply plunge the tomatoes into boiling water for 1 minute, drain, refresh and peel the skin.

Holding each tomato with tongs or a skewer, char them over a gas flame until the skins blister and start to shrivel. Peel off the skins, chop the flesh and put into a bowl. Add the oil, chillies, garlic, basil, sugar, salt and pepper and leave to infuse while you cook the pasta (or longer if possible).

Bring a large saucepan of salted water to the boil. Add the pasta and cook until al dente, or according to the instructions on the packet. Drain well and immediately stir in the fresh tomato sauce. Serve at once with the grated cheese.

roasted tomato sauce

There are few dishes more simple and yet tasty than a sauce made of fresh tomatoes enhanced with a little garlic, chilli, olive oil and herbs. This rich tomato sauce can be served with spaghetti, as part of vegetable lasagne, or as a pizza topping, and also provide the base for soups or stews.

1 kg vine-ripened tomatoes, roughly chopped

2 tablespoons extra virgin olive oil

2 garlic cloves, crushed

grated zest of 1 unwaxed lemon

a pinch of dried chilli flakes

2 tablespoons chopped basil

sea salt and freshly ground black pepper

SERVES 4

Preheat the oven to 230°C (450°F) Gas 8.

Put the tomatoes, oil, garlic, lemon zest, chilli flakes and seasoning in a single layer in a roasting tin. Toss well. Roast for 45 minutes, or until the tomatoes are browned and the juices have reduced down to a glaze.

Transfer the tomatoes and all the pan juices to a deep bowl, add the basil and, using a hand-blender, purée until smooth. Season to taste. Serve hot with some freshly cooked pasta or leave to cool in a plastic container.

Note During the summer months, when tomatoes are plentiful and at their best, make up several quantities of this sauce and freeze for use in the winter.

This pasta recipe involves the Italian technique of gently blanching the garlic in warm oil so that it softens and imparts its flavour without dominating the other fresh ingredients. When it comes to tomatoes, we are spoilt for choice during the summer months, so use a number of interesting varieties, heirloom if possible, and mix up the colours. The bitter red endive leaves offset the fruity sweetness of the tomatoes.

linguine with heirloom tomatoes, red endive and black olives

65 ml olive oil

4 garlic cloves, chopped

6 medium tomatoes, roughly chopped

1 red Belgian endive (chicory), leaves torn

1 tablespoon of small black olives

400 g dried linguine

50 g Parmesan cheese, finely grated

sea salt and freshly ground black pepper

SERVES 4

Heat the oil in a large frying pan, add the garlic and cook over medium heat for a couple of minutes, to soften, but don't let it burn. Add the tomatoes to the pan and cook for 2–3 minutes so that they are just soft and starting to break up. Remove from the heat, stir through the endive leaves and olives and season with salt and pepper. Set aside.

Bring a large saucepan of salted water to the boil. Add the pasta and cook until al dente, or according to the instructions on the packet. Drain well and put in a large bowl. Add the tomato sauce and half of the Parmesan and toss to combine. Divide between 4 serving plates or bowls and serve immediately with the remaining Parmesan sprinkled on top.

tomato sauce
with double basil

3 tablespoons olive oil

2 garlic cloves, finely chopped

1 shallot, finely chopped

25 g basil leaves

500 g ripe tomatoes, coarsely chopped, or 400 g tinned plum tomatoes

a pinch of sugar

350 g dried pasta, such as spaghetti or linguine

sea salt and freshly ground black pepper

freshly grated Parmesan cheese

crispy breadcrumbs, to serve (optional)

SERVES 4

In summer, make this with fragrant ripe tomatoes – otherwise, use tinned Italian plum tomatoes. The basil is added in two stages: first for depth of flavour, then at the end for a burst of fresh fragrance, hence the name double basil.

Heat the oil in a saucepan and add the garlic, shallot and half the basil. Cook for 3–4 minutes until the shallot is golden.

Add the tomatoes and cook, stirring, for 10 minutes, until thickened and pulpy. Add the sugar, 100 ml water and salt and pepper to taste. Bring to the boil, cover and simmer very gently for 1 hour until dark red and thickened, with droplets of oil on the surface.

Towards the end of the cooking time for the sauce, bring a large saucepan of salted water to the boil. Add the pasta and cook until al dente, or according to the instructions on the packet.

Tear the remaining basil into the tomato sauce and add the sauce to the drained pasta. Toss to mix, then serve topped with Parmesan and crispy breadcrumbs, if desired.

Variation Crispy breadcrumbs make a great addition to any tomato-based pasta sauce. Heat a couple of tablespoons of olive oil in a frying pan and add a good tablespoon or two of fresh white breadcrumbs. Cook over high heat, stirring, until golden brown. The smaller crumbs will char a little at the bottom of the pan, but that's good. Serve straight from the pan, sprinkled on top of the pasta, while the crumbs are still hot and sizzling.

roasted vegetable sauce with capers and cherry tomatoes

1 small aubergine, about 100 g

1 red pepper, halved and deseeded

1 yellow pepper, halved and deseeded

100 g courgettes

100 g leeks, split and well washed

1½ tablespoons finely chopped rosemary

2 garlic cloves, finely chopped

2 tablespoons olive oil

400 g dried pasta, such as ridged penne or tubetti

1–2 tablespoons capers, rinsed and drained

100 g cherry tomatoes

extra virgin olive oil, to serve

6 sprigs of rosemary, to serve

freshly grated Parmesan cheese, to serve

SERVES 4

When choosing peppers, aubergines and courgettes, squeeze them lightly to ensure the flesh is firm. When buying leeks, look for a good proportion of white trunk, the really tender, sweet part. The leaves needn't be wasted, however – provided they are fresh, just cut them off and use them to make stock.

Preheat the oven to 200°C (400°F) Gas 6.

Cut the aubergine, peppers, courgettes and leeks into bite-sized pieces, about 2 cm square, and arrange in a single layer in a roasting tin. Add the rosemary, garlic and oil and mix well with your hands. Cover with foil, transfer to the preheated oven and roast for 20–30 minutes until tender.

Remove and discard the foil, add the capers and cherry tomatoes, stir well and roast for a further 10 minutes.

Meanwhile, bring a large saucepan of salted water to the boil. Add the pasta and cook until al dente, or according to the instructions on the packet.

Add the roasted vegetables to the drained pasta, stir well and spread out on a serving plate. Sprinkle with oil and rosemary and serve with Parmesan.

Variation Instead of cherry tomatoes, add 3 tablespoons black olives.

tagliatelle with sun-blush tomatoes and toasted pine nuts

2 tablespoons pine nuts

200 g dried tagliatelle

2 tablespoons olive oil

2 garlic cloves, finely chopped

100 g sun-blush tomatoes in oil (or marinated in oil, garlic and oregano), roughly chopped

120 g fresh spinach, stalks removed and leaves shredded

10 pitted black olives, halved

sea salt and freshly ground black pepper

Parmesan cheese shavings, to serve

SERVES 2

Satisfyingly quick to make and light to eat, the vitamin C in this dish will help with the absorption of iron found in the spinach.

Put the pine nuts in a dry frying pan and toast for a few minutes, turning occasionally, until light golden – keep an eye on them, as they burn easily.

Bring a large saucepan of salted water to the boil. Add the pasta and cook until al dente, or according to the instructions on the packet. Drain, reserving 120 ml of the cooking water.

Heat the oil in a frying pan and add the garlic, sun-blush tomatoes and spinach. Fry, stirring continuously, for 2–3 minutes until the spinach has wilted.

Add the olives, pasta and reserved cooking water. Season well and toss thoroughly over low heat until heated through and combined.

Transfer to 2 serving plates or bowls and serve sprinkled with the Parmesan shavings, plus salt and pepper to taste.

puttanesca

2 tablespoons olive oil

1 onion, finely chopped

2 garlic cloves, finely chopped

4 anchovy fillets in oil, drained
and coarsely chopped

2 red chillies, finely chopped

4 ripe tomatoes, coarsely chopped

1 tablespoon capers, rinsed and
drained

100 ml red wine

350 g dried pasta, such as gemelli
or penne

75 g small black olives

2 tablespoons chopped
flat leaf parsley

freshly ground black pepper

freshly grated Parmesan cheese,
to serve

SERVES 4

Puttanesca sauce was famously named in honour
of the ladies of the night, although no one seems
quite sure why. This robust dish goes perfectly with
a bottle of full-bodied red wine.

Heat the oil in a saucepan, then add the onion, garlic, anchovies
and chillies. Cook over medium heat for 4–5 minutes until softened
and golden. Add the tomatoes. Cook for 3–4 minutes, stirring
occasionally, until softened.

Add the capers, wine and black pepper to taste, then cover and
simmer for 20 minutes.

Meanwhile, bring a large saucepan of salted water to the boil. Add
the pasta and cook until al dente, or according to the instructions
on the packet.

Add the tomato sauce, olives and parsley to the pasta in its warm
pan and toss to mix. Divide between 4 serving plates or bowls and
serve topped with grated Parmesan.

aglio, olio e peperoncino

350 g dried pasta, such spaghettini or penne

150 ml very best olive oil

4 garlic cloves, peeled but whole

1 small to medium dried chilli (to taste), finely chopped

2 tablespoons finely chopped parsley

freshly grated Parmesan cheese (optional), to serve

SERVES 4–6 AS A STARTER

If you like spicy and simple food, this is for you. It is a typical dish of the mountainous Abruzzo region, where long snowy winters have inspired all kinds of warming specialities.

Bring a large saucepan of salted water to the boil. Add the pasta and cook until al dente, or according to the instructions on the packet. Meanwhile, slowly heat the oil in a frying pan with the garlic and chilli. When the garlic turns golden, discard it. Drain the pasta, then return it to the saucepan. Add the hot flavoured oil and chopped parsley and stir well. Serve at once, with Parmesan, if using.

Variations
Arrabbiata
For spice lovers, this is a tomato-based version of the above recipe. The word arrabbiata translates as 'angry' from Italian. It is a popular dish in Rome and generally made on demand in simple eateries. Use the Tomato with Double Basil Sauce recipe on page 119, but halve the amount of basil and double the amount of garlic and chillies. Add 2 tablespoons finely chopped parsley at the end.

Amatriciana
This sauce is very similar to Arrabbiata, but contains an onion instead of garlic and has a pancetta base. It is featured in the meat and poultry section on page 70.

farfalle pasta with asparagus, soft-boiled duck eggs and Parmesan

4 duck eggs or 6 hens' eggs

2 bunches of thin asparagus spears

2 tablespoons olive oil

2 garlic cloves, chopped

250 ml single cream

400 g dried farfalle or pasta of your choice

50 g Parmesan cheese, finely grated

2 handfuls of wild rocket leaves

sea salt and freshly ground black pepper

SERVES 4

You can, of course, use hens' eggs here, but duck eggs are a bit of a treat and can easily be found at farmers' markets. They are slightly larger and have a rich flavour. Do use fine asparagus for this recipe – fresh and tender young spears grown locally are best as, once picked, their sweetness fades fast.

Put the eggs in a saucepan and pour in sufficient cold water to cover. Bring to the boil over high heat and cook for 5 minutes. Drain and run the eggs under cold water until the shells are cool enough to handle. Set aside.

Trim or snap any woody ends off the asparagus and cut the spears into 2-cm lengths. Put the oil in a frying pan set over high heat. Add the asparagus and cook for 2 minutes, stirring constantly. Next, add the garlic and cook for another minute, before adding the cream to the pan. Remove from the heat and leave to sit so that the garlic flavours the cream.

Bring a large saucepan of salted water to the boil. Add the pasta and cook until al dente, or according to the packet instructions. Drain and return it to the warm pan. Add the asparagus sauce. Peel and roughly chop the eggs. The yolks will be soft, so quickly add these to the warm pasta along with the Parmesan and rocket. Season well with salt and pepper and stir gently to combine. Divide between 4 serving plates or bowls and serve immediately.

pasta primavera

500 g green vegetables, such as green beans, asparagus, peas, broad beans or a mixture (shelled weight)

2 tablespoons olive oil

1 onion, finely chopped

2 tablespoons white wine

400 g ripe tomatoes, skinned, deseeded and chopped

1 tablespoon finely chopped mint

1 tablespoon finely chopped basil

400 g dried pasta of your choice

3 tablespoons freshly grated Parmesan cheese

80 g Parma ham, cut into strips (optional)

sea salt and freshly ground black pepper

basil leaves, to serve

SERVES 4

Vegetables need little cooking or adornment if they are young, sweet and fresh. Harvest periods are short, so relish each vegetable in its season and reinvent this recipe as the seasons change.

Prepare the green vegetables. If using asparagus or green beans, trim them and cut them into 2–3-cm lengths. Heat the oil gently in a frying pan. Add the onion and fry gently until softened and translucent. Add the wine and let bubble until evaporated. Stir in the green vegetables and tomatoes, then season to taste. Stir again, cover and cook for 10–20 minutes or until tender. Stir in the herbs, then taste again for seasoning.

Towards the end of the cooking time for the sauce bring a large saucepan of salted water to the boil. Add the pasta and cook until al dente, or according to the instructions on the packet. Add the sauce to the pasta, then add the Parmesan and strips of Parma ham, if using. Stir well and serve topped with basil leaves.

Variations
• Try young carrots with spring cabbage, 1 teaspoon crushed juniper berries and 1 teaspoon chopped thyme.

• Omit the Parma ham and use 50 g sun-dried tomatoes, thinly sliced, 1½ tablespoons capers and 1½ tablespoons olives.

• Omit the Parma ham and add 1 tablespoon finely chopped anchovies, the finely grated zest of 1 small unwaxed lemon and 1 tablespoon finely chopped parsley.

roasted aubergine and tomato sauce

2 aubergines, cut into 3-cm cubes

500 g ripe tomatoes, quartered

2 garlic cloves, halved

4 tablespoons olive oil

300 g dried pasta, such as fusilli
or fusilli bucati

1 shallot, finely chopped

2 tablespoons chopped mint

2 tablespoons chopped
coriander

freshly squeezed juice of 1 lime

sea salt and freshly ground
black pepper

SERVES 4

Aubergine is the key ingredient here and gives the sauce a lovely, meaty consistency. The addition of mint and lime adds a flavoursome twist.

Preheat the oven to 200°C (400°F) Gas 6.

Put the aubergines, tomatoes and garlic into a roasting tin. Add 2 tablespoons of the oil and mix. Sprinkle with salt and pepper and cook in the preheated oven for 30–40 minutes, occasionally turning the vegetables, until the aubergines are tender and golden.

Meanwhile, bring a large saucepan of salted water to the boil. Add the pasta and cook until al dente, or according to the instructions on the packet. Drain well.

Return the pasta to the warm pan. Add the roasted aubergines and tomatoes, then the shallot, mint, coriander and lime juice. Add the remaining oil and toss well to mix. Divide between 4 serving plates or bowls and serve immediately.

chilli and black bean sauce
with garlic-fried breadcrumbs

400 g tinned black beans, drained
and rinsed

2 tablespoons olive oil

1 carrot, finely chopped

1 small onion, finely chopped

½ celery stick, finely chopped

2 garlic cloves, crushed

400 g tinned plum tomatoes,
drained (reserve the juice),
deseeded and chopped

a small piece of dried chilli
or ½ cinnamon stick

250 g dried pasta, such as small
tubetti, spirali or penne

50 g rocket

sea salt and freshly ground
black pepper

50 g Parmesan cheese shavings,
to serve

garlic-fried breadcrumbs

3 tablespoons olive oil

25 g fresh breadcrumbs

1 teaspoon finely chopped
rosemary

1 garlic clove, finely chopped

SERVES 4–6 AS A STARTER

Black beans make a nutritious and satisfying pasta topping. They go perfectly with a tasty tomato sauce and garlicky breadcrumbs.

Heat the oil gently in a saucepan. Add the carrot, onion, celery, garlic and beans and stir gently in the oil for 5 minutes, or until the vegetables soften. Add the tomatoes and chilli or cinnamon and stir again. Heat to simmering, cover with a lid and cook over very low heat for 30 minutes, stirring from time to time. You might need to add a little reserved tomato juice to keep the sauce moist. Add salt and pepper to taste and discard the chilli or cinnamon stick.

Towards the end of the cooking time for the sauce, bring a large saucepan of salted water to the boil. Add the pasta, and cook until al dente, or according to the instructions on the packet. Drain well.

To make the garlic-fried breadcrumbs, heat the oil in a frying pan. Put the breadcrumbs, rosemary and garlic in a bowl and mix well. Add the mixture to the pan and fry until crisp and golden. Transfer to a plate lined with kitchen paper, leave to drain and cool.

Add the sauce and rocket to the pasta and stir well. Serve topped with the breadcrumbs and Parmesan shavings.

calabrese and broccoli arabesque

400 g dried pasta, such as spaghettini or orecchiette

50 g pine nuts, plus extra to serve

50 g sultanas

750 g brassica vegetables, such as cauliflower, separated into florets, or purple sprouting broccoli or a mixture

1½ tablespoons tomato purée

100 ml warm water

100 ml olive oil

1 onion, finely sliced

1 small tin anchovies, about 50 g, drained thoroughly and patted dry with kitchen paper

50 ml scalding hot milk

torn coriander leaves or flat leaf parsley, to serve

freshly grated pecorino or Parmesan cheese, to serve

SERVES 4

This unusual sauce, enhanced with sultanas, pine nuts and anchovies, explodes with flavour. It is based on a classic recipe popular in parts of southern Italy and Sicily, where ingredients such as sultanas and pine nuts show an Arab influence – arabesque. You can also serve it as a side dish with meat or fish.

Put the pine nuts in a dry frying pan and heat gently until golden brown all over. Take care, because they burn easily. Let cool.

Soak the sultanas in boiling water for 15 minutes, then drain and pat dry with kitchen paper. Cook the cauliflower and/or broccoli in a large saucepan of boiling salted water until just soft, 5–10 minutes. Drain well.

Meanwhile, bring another large saucepan of salted water to the boil. Add the pasta and cook until al dente, or according to the instructions on the packet. Drain well.

Put the tomato purée in a small bowl, add the warm water and stir to dilute. Heat half the oil in a frying pan, then add the onion and tomato purée mixture. Cook over low heat until softened, then add the boiled vegetables.

Mash the anchovies in a small bowl, then stir in the hot milk and remaining oil to form a smooth paste. Pour over the vegetables, add the sultanas and pine nuts, stir well and cover with a lid. Turn off the heat and set aside to develop the flavours.

Add the sauce to the pasta, stir well, then transfer to a large serving dish. Add the coriander and extra pine nuts. Serve at once with grated pecorino.

spaghetti with broccoli, walnuts and ricotta

The light texture and creamy flavour of ricotta cheese makes the perfect backdrop to walnuts and broccoli in this deliciously simple and quick pasta dish.

100 g walnut halves

1 head of broccoli, about 400–500 g

3 tablespoons olive oil

3 garlic cloves, thinly sliced

1 tablespoon chopped flat leaf parsley

finely grated zest and freshly squeezed juice of 1 unwaxed lemon

200 g ricotta cheese

400 g dried spaghetti

sea salt and freshly ground black pepper

SERVES 4

Preheat the oven to 180°C (350°F) Gas 4.

Spread the walnuts out on a baking tray and oven-roast for about 8 minutes, shaking the tray occasionally, until they start to brown.

To prepare the broccoli, trim off the gnarly part, about 2 cm from the stem end, and discard. Thinly slice the stem until you reach the point where it starts to branch into florets. Slice off the individual florets. Heat the oil in a frying pan, add the stems and cook for about 2–3 minutes, turning often, then add the florets and cook for about 5 minutes, until the broccoli has softened. Add the garlic, parsley, lemon zest and walnuts and cook for 5 minutes, stirring often. Reduce the heat to medium and stir through the ricotta and lemon juice. Season well and leave in the pan to keep warm.

Meanwhile, bring a large saucepan of salted water to the boil. Add the pasta and cook until al dente, or according to the instructions on the packet. Drain and return it to the warm pan with the sauce. Stir gently to combine and serve immediately.

tossed courgette ribbons and pasta

400 g dried pappardelle pasta

200 g courgettes, very thinly sliced lengthways

finely grated zest and freshly squeezed juice of 1 unwaxed lemon

2 tablespoons extra virgin olive oil

a bunch of chives, finely chopped

sea salt and freshly ground black pepper

SERVES 4

This dish is very quick to make and relies on just a few key ingredients. It goes extremely well with grilled fish or meat.

Bring a large saucepan of salted water to the boil. Add the pasta and cook until al dente, or according to the packet instructions. Add the courgette to the pasta for the final 3 minutes of cooking.

Put the lemon zest and juice into a bowl, add the oil and mix. Add the chives, salt and pepper.

Drain the pasta and courgettes and return them to the pan. Add the lemon juice mixture and toss well to coat. Divide between 4 serving plates or bowls and serve immediately.

spaghetti with chilli courgette crumbs

400 g dried spaghetti or similar pasta

90 ml olive oil

100 g fresh breadcrumbs

8 small or baby courgettes, cut into julienne strips

2 garlic cloves, grated

2 small red chillies, deseeded and chopped

finely grated Parmesan cheese, to serve

SERVES 4

This is one of those pasta combinations that works with just about any of your favourite seasonings. You can easily use chilli flakes instead of fresh chillies or throw in a few chopped anchovies. When it comes to the flavour of courgettes, size does matter. Like most green vegetables, the younger, the tastier, so use small ones here, no longer than 15 cm, for a really simple yet delicious pasta sauce. And do use good bread, even if it is stale. The flavour of a loaf intensifies as it becomes stale and a cheap white loaf will always make really nasty, cheap, white crumbs.

Bring a large saucepan of salted water to the boil. Add the pasta and cook until al dente, or according to the packet instructions. Drain well and return to the pan to keep warm.

Meanwhile, heat a large frying pan over medium heat. When it is hot, add half the oil, swirling around to coat the pan, then add the breadcrumbs. Cook the crumbs for 3–4 minutes, stirring constantly until evenly browned with a nutty aroma. Remove from the pan and wipe the pan clean.

Add the remaining oil to the pan and cook the courgettes for 5 minutes over high heat, turning often, until golden and starting to crisp up. Add the garlic and chillies and cook for 4–5 minutes, stirring often.

Add the cooked pasta and breadcrumbs to the pan, tossing around to combine. Serve immediately with grated Parmesan sprinkled over the top.

courgette and toasted pine nut pasta

1 tablespoon pine nuts, about 25 g

400 g dried spaghettini

100 ml good olive oil

1 garlic clove, peeled but left whole

400 g baby courgettes, thinly sliced

sea salt and freshly ground
black pepper

1 tablespoon finely chopped parsley

SERVES 4

This recipe hails from Sicily, where regional cooking abounds with vegetable-based recipes enhanced by the island's glorious olive oil. The quality of the oil is as important as the freshness of the courgettes in this dish, so use something special when making it.

Put the pine nuts in a dry frying pan and heat gently until golden brown all over. Take care because they burn easily. Leave to cool.

Bring a large saucepan of salted water to the boil. Add the pasta and cook until al dente, or according to the instructions on the packet. Drain well.

Meanwhile, heat the olive oil and garlic in a large frying pan and, when the garlic starts to turn golden, discard it. Add the courgettes and stir-fry quickly until golden. Add salt and pepper to taste.

Add the courgettes and their cooking oil to the freshly cooked pasta. Stir well, sprinkle with the parsley and the toasted pine nuts and serve immediately.

pappardelle pasta with roast fennel, tomato and olives

65 ml extra virgin olive oil

4 tomatoes, halved

2 red onions, cut into wedges

4 small courgettes, thickly sliced

2 small fennel bulbs, thickly sliced

2 garlic cloves, thickly sliced

1 teaspoon smoked paprika (pimentón)

50 g small black olives

400 g fresh pappardelle pasta or Fresh Pasta Dough (page 12)

2 tablespoons butter

sea salt and freshly ground black pepper

grated manchego cheese, to serve

SERVES 4

Roasting vegetables in the oven makes easy work of a pasta sauce. The vegetables soften and sweeten while they cook and there is no constant stirring involved as there is with hob-top cooking. This recipes calls for fresh pasta. Time permitting, you could always make your own pappardelle following the recipe on page 12 and freeze any leftover strands.

Preheat the oven to 220°C (425°F) Gas 7.

Put the oil in a roasting tin and heat in the oven for 5 minutes.

Add all of the vegetables and the garlic to the roasting tin and sprinkle over the paprika. Season to taste with salt and pepper. Roast in the preheated oven for about 20 minutes, giving the tin a shake after 15 minutes. Remove from the oven and stir in the olives. Cover and leave to sit while you cook the pasta.

Bring a large saucepan of salted water to the boil. Add the pasta and cook according to the packet instructions, or just until the pasta rises to the surface – it will cook much quicker than dried pasta. Drain well and return to the warm pan. Add the butter and toss well. Add the roasted vegetables and toss gently to combine. Sprinkle with grated manchego to serve.

mushroom and thyme ragu with hand-torn pasta

2 tablespoons olive oil

2 tablespoons unsalted butter

1 onion, chopped

2 garlic cloves, chopped

3 large field mushrooms, caps removed and cut into 2-cm pieces

200 g button mushrooms

100 g fresh shiitake mushrooms, quartered

3 sprigs thyme

250 ml red wine

1 cinnamon stick

250 ml vegetable or beef stock

400 g fresh lasagne sheets, or Fresh Pasta Dough (page 12) cut or torn into thick strips

sea salt and freshly ground black pepper

freshly grated Parmesan cheese, to serve

SERVES 4

Many exotic mushroom varieties can be bought year-round, offering a constant supply of just about any mushroom you could wish for. Here, a mixture has been used, including meaty field mushrooms as they go hand in hand with the other comforting, rich flavours like fresh thyme, red wine and cinnamon.

Heat the oil and butter in a heavy-based saucepan over medium heat. Add the onion and garlic and cook for 4–5 minutes, until the onions have softened. Increase the heat to high, add the mushrooms and thyme and cook for a further 8–10 minutes, stirring often, until the mushrooms darken and soften.

Add the red wine and cinnamon to the pan and boil for 5 minutes. Pour in the stock and season well. Reduce the heat and gently simmer the mixture for 35–40 minutes.

Bring a large saucepan of salted water to the boil. Add the pasta and cook according to the packet instructions, or just until the pasta rises to the surface. Drain well and divide between 4 serving plates or bowls. Remove the cinnamon stick from the mushroom sauce then spoon on top of the pasta, sprinkle with Parmesan and serve immediately.

pappardelle with portobello mushrooms

200 g fresh chestnuts (optional)

1 tablespoon olive oil

15 g butter

2 garlic cloves, chopped

400 g portobello or field mushrooms, sliced

2 sprigs thyme

125 ml dry white wine

250 ml single cream

1 bunch of chives, cut into 3-cm lengths

50 g pecorino cheese, finely grated, plus extra to serve

400 g dried pappardelle, tagliatelle or any other ribbon pasta

sea salt and freshly ground black pepper

SERVES 4

Fresh chestnuts aren't always easy to find, but if you can get your hands on some, they really do make a wonderful addition to this pasta dish, giving it a slightly festive flavour. Don't feel too guilty about the cream – the chestnuts are low in fat and calories.

Preheat the oven to 200°C (400°F) Gas 6.

Score a cross on one end of each chestnut. Put them on a baking tray and roast in the preheated oven for 10–15 minutes, until the skins split. Remove and leave to cool then pull off the shells, and rub away the fleshy skin underneath. Set aside.

Put the oil and butter in a frying pan set over high heat. When the butter sizzles, add the garlic and cook for just 1 minute, making sure it doesn't burn. Add the mushrooms and thyme, reduce the heat to medium and partially cover with a lid. Cook for 10 minutes, stirring often. Add the wine to the pan and simmer until the liquid is reduced by half. Add the cream, reduce the heat and cook for 15 minutes, until the mixture thickens. Add the chives and half of the pecorino and stir to combine. Season to taste with salt and pepper. Take off the heat and cover with foil to keep warm.

Bring a large saucepan of salted water to the boil. Add the pasta and cook until al dente, or according to the instructions on the packet. Drain well and return to the pan to keep warm. Add the mushroom sauce along with the chestnuts, if using, gently toss to mix and serve immediately with extra pecorino for sprinkling.

This tasty pasta dish is inspired by the classic pumpkin-filled ravioli with sage butter. This inside-out version is much easier to make. Butternut squash has been used here, but you could use any winter squash, including pumpkin.

spaghetti with butternut squash, sage and pecorino

65 ml olive oil

400 g butternut squash, peeled, deseeded and cut into thin wedges

2 garlic cloves, chopped

10–12 small sage leaves

400 g dried spaghetti

1 tablespoon chopped flat leaf parsley

50 g pecorino cheese, grated

sea salt and freshly ground black pepper

SERVES 4

Put the oil in a frying pan set over high heat. Add the squash and cook for 5–6 minutes, turning often, until golden but not breaking up. Add the garlic and sage to the pan and cook for 2–3 minutes. Remove from the heat and leave to allow the flavours to develop.

Bring a large saucepan of salted water to the boil. Add the pasta and cook until al dente, or according to the instructions on the packet. Drain well and return to the warm pan. Add the squash mixture, the parsley and half of the pecorino and season well. Divide between 4 serving plates or bowls, sprinkle with the remaining pecorino and serve.

tagliatelle with pan-fried pumpkin and red pepper oil

1 small red pepper, sliced

6 large red chillies, sliced

1 small red onion, sliced

4 garlic cloves, peeled but left whole

1 teaspoon cumin seeds

65 ml olive oil

1 tablespoon light olive oil

400 g pumpkin or butternut squash, peeled, deseeded and chopped into 2–3-cm pieces

400 g dried pappardelle, tagliatelle or any other ribbon pasta

finely grated zest and juice of 1 unwaxed lemon

50 g wild rocket leaves

2 tablespoons chopped flat leaf parsley

sea salt and freshly ground black pepper

SERVES 4

The trick to this recipe is to take it slowly. Allow the red pepper and chillies to gently release their colour and flavour into the oil by roasting them in a low oven for a full hour.

Preheat the oven to 180°C (350°F) Gas 4.

Put the red pepper, chillies, onion, garlic, cumin seeds and 2 tablespoons of the olive oil in a roasting tin. Cook in the preheated oven for 1 hour, turning often. Transfer the contents of the roasting tin to a food processor while still hot. Add the remaining oil and whizz until smooth. Leave to cool, then pour the mixture into a clean and dry screwtop jar.

Heat the light olive oil in a frying pan set over high heat and add the pumpkin. Cook for 10 minutes, turning often, until each piece is golden brown all over. Meanwhile, bring a large saucepan of salted water to the boil. Add the pasta and cook until al dente, or according to the instructions on the packet. Drain well and put in a large bowl. Add 2–3 tablespoons of the red pepper oil. Add the cooked pumpkin, lemon zest and juice, rocket and parsley and toss to combine. Season and serve immediately.

Note The remaining red pepper oil will keep for 1 week when stored in an airtight jar in the refrigerator. It can be added to tomato-based sauces for extra flavour.

pasta with pan-fried squash, walnut and parsley sauce

150 g fresh walnut halves

2–3 fat garlic cloves, peeled but left whole

5 tablespoons olive oil

1 tablespoon walnut oil

5 tablespoons double cream or crème fraîche

2 tablespoons chopped flat leaf parsley

650 g prepared squash, cut into 1-cm thick slices or chunks

1–2 pinches dried chilli flakes, crushed

400 g dried pasta of your choice

sea salt and freshly ground black pepper

freshly grated Parmesan, to serve

freshly squeezed lemon juice, to taste

freshly grated nutmeg, to taste

SERVES 4

This is a lovely and unusual pasta dish, well suited to autumn, when walnuts and all kinds of orange-fleshed squashes are at their best. In northern Italy, a version of this walnut sauce is traditionally served with pappardelle pasta, but it is good with other shapes too, including, strange as it may seem (and distinctly unItalian), wholemeal spaghetti.

Preheat the oven to 180°C (350°F) Gas 4.

Put the walnuts on a baking tray and toast them in the preheated oven for 5–6 minutes, making sure they don't burn. Turn them onto a dry, clean tea towel and rub vigorously to remove as much of the skin as possible. Chop 50 g of the nuts roughly and set aside. Put the remaining 100 g in a food processor. Blanch the garlic in boiling water for 2–3 minutes, drain and rinse. Put the garlic in the processor with the walnuts, add 2 tablespoons olive oil, the walnut oil and cream. Whizz to make a paste. Set aside a third of the parsley, then whizz the remaining two-thirds into the sauce. Chop the reserved parsley and set aside, along with the sauce.

In a large frying pan, heat the remaining oil over medium heat, add the squash and chilli flakes and cook, turning the squash now and then, until it is tender and lightly browned, about 10–12 minutes. Meanwhile, bring a large saucepan of salted water to the boil. Add the pasta and cook until al dente, or according to the instructions on the packet.

When the pasta is cooked, drain, reserving 4–5 tablespoons of the cooking water. Add enough of this water into the sauce to make it creamy, then season with salt, pepper and a little nutmeg. Toss the pasta with the squash, remaining walnuts and parsley and a little of the sauce. Serve the Parmesan and remaining sauce at the table.

foaming sage butter

125 g unsalted butter

2 tablespoons chopped sage

2 garlic cloves, crushed

sea salt and freshly ground
black pepper

SERVES 2

This is so simple, yet totally delicious – melted butter
is sautéed until golden and nutty, then mixed with
fresh sage leaves and a little crushed garlic. It is
particularly good with pumpkin ravioli or spinach
and ricotta gnocchi.

Melt the butter in a small frying pan, then cook over medium heat
for 3–4 minutes until it turns golden brown. Remove the pan from
the heat and add the sage leaves, garlic and a little seasoning.
Leave to sizzle in the butter for 30 seconds until fragrant.

roasted squash, feta and sage sauce

500 g butternut squash flesh, diced

1 small red onion, thinly sliced

1 tablespoon chopped sage

5 tablespoons extra virgin olive oil

4 garlic cloves, finely chopped

a pinch of dried chilli flakes

50 g pine nuts

200 g feta cheese, diced

sea salt and freshly ground
black pepper

SERVES 4

Roasting the squash and onion first adds a slightly
smoky flavour to this pasta sauce. You can use either
butternut squash or pumpkin – in either case you
will need a 750-g vegetable to yield 500 g of flesh.

Preheat the oven to 220°C (425°F) Gas 7.

Put the squash, onion, sage, 1 tablespoon of the oil and some
seasoning in a roasting tin, toss well and roast for 30 minutes,
or until the vegetables are golden and cooked through.

Heat the remaining oil in a large frying pan and gently fry the
garlic, chilli flakes and a little seasoning for 2–3 minutes until soft,
but not browned. Add the pine nuts and stir-fry for 2–3 minutes
until lightly browned. Add the roasted squash, onions, sage and
the feta, and stir well until combined. Serve at once.

pappardelle
with basil oil

350 g dried pappardelle

6 tablespoons extra virgin olive oil

2 garlic cloves, chopped

1 handful fresh chives, chervil, dill or parsley, plus extra to serve (optional)

2 large handfuls basil leaves

4 tablespoons flaked almonds

4 tablespoons freshly grated pecorino or Parmesan cheese

sea salt and freshly ground black pepper

SERVES 4

Wide ribbon pasta is particularly popular in Tuscany and also in Umbria. It is frequently served with rich meat and game sauces, but freshly made basil oil dressing is a superb alternative. Eat this dish on its own, as a starter, or use as an accompaniment.

Bring a large saucepan of salted water to the boil. Add the pasta and cook until al dente, or according to the packet instructions.

Meanwhile, heat half the oil in a frying pan, add the garlic, chives and one handful of the basil leaves. Sauté for 1–1½ minutes or until the greens have wilted and the garlic has become aromatic.

Transfer to a blender or food processor and blend to a paste. Pour into a plastic or stainless steel (non-reactive) sieve set over a bowl. Press all the oil through with the back of a ladle or wooden spoon.

Heat the remaining oil in the frying pan, add the almonds and fry until golden.

Drain the cooked pasta and add it to the pan with the almonds and the basil oil. Add the remaining basil leaves, the cheese and extra chives, if using. Season to taste and serve the pasta hot or warm.

Variation Instead of straining the basil mixture, just stir it through the cooked pasta for added texture.

tapenade

125 g niçoise olives, stoned

2 anchovy fillets in oil, drained

2 garlic cloves, crushed

2 tablespoons capers

1 teaspoon Dijon mustard

4 tablespoons extra virgin olive oil

freshly squeezed lemon juice to taste

freshly ground black pepper

MAKES APPROXIMATELY 150 ML

Using niçoise olives will give the finished sauce a truly authentic flavour. It is preferable to buy whole olives and stone them yourself – to do this, simply press down firmly on the olives using your thumb, and the olive flesh will split to reveal the stone, which is then discarded.

Put the olives, anchovies, garlic, capers and mustard in a mortar (or food processor) and pound with a pestle to form a fairly smooth paste. Gradually blend in the oil and add lemon juice and pepper to taste. Transfer to a dish, cover and refrigerate for up to 5 days.

pesto

50 g basil leaves

1 garlic clove, crushed

2 tablespoons pine nuts

a pinch of sea salt

6–8 tablespoons extra virgin olive oil

2 tablespoons freshly grated Parmesan cheese

freshly ground black pepper

MAKES APPROXIMATELY 150 ML

Over the past 20 years, this thick, aromatic herb and nut sauce from Genoa has travelled widely and is now used by cooks throughout the world to serve with pasta or grilled fish, or to be stirred into soup.

Put the basil, garlic, pine nuts and salt in a mortar (or food processor) and pound with a pestle to form a fairly smooth paste. Add the oil slowly until you reach a texture that is soft but not runny. Add the Parmesan and pepper to taste. Cover the surface with a little more oil. Refrigerate for up to 3 days.

Tip If you make this sauce in a food processor, do not over-process, otherwise the sauce will be too smooth.

walnut and caper pesto

Fresh walnuts have a rich creamy texture which emulsifies the pesto beautifully. If you can, try using a traditional mezzaluna for chopping – it makes light work of herbs.

2 garlic cloves, peeled but left whole

85 g walnut halves, fresh if possible

2 tablespoons capers

50 g flat leaf parsley leaves

200 ml extra virgin olive oil, plus extra for preserving

50 g unsalted butter, softened

4 tablespoons freshly grated pecorino cheese

sea salt and freshly ground black pepper

SERVES 4–6

Put the garlic, walnuts, capers and a little salt in a mortar, then pound with a pestle until broken up. Add the parsley, a few leaves at a time, pounding and mixing to a thick paste. Gradually beat in the oil until creamy and thick. Beat in the butter, season with pepper, then beat in the pecorino. Alternatively, blend all of the ingredients in a food processor or blender until smooth.

Store in a jar, with a layer of olive oil on top to exclude the air, in the refrigerator until needed, for up to 2 weeks. Level the surface each time you use it, and re-cover with olive oil.

broccoli and pine nut pesto

175 g dried pasta, such as penne or fusilli

175 g broccoli, cut into florets

2 tablespoons pine nuts

3 tablespoons olive oil

3 garlic cloves, finely chopped

1 red chilli, deseeded and finely chopped

freshly squeezed juice of ½ lemon

fresh shavings of Parmesan cheese, to serve

sea salt and freshly ground black pepper

SERVES 2

The combination of broccoli and pine nuts makes for a flavoursome pasta dish with a lovely texture. For an added kick, be a little more liberal with the chilli.

Bring a large saucepan of salted water to the boil. Add the pasta and cook until al dente, or according to the packet instructions.

Cook the broccoli in a separate saucepan of boiling, salted water for 10–12 minutes until very soft. Meanwhile, heat a dry frying pan until hot, add the pine nuts and cook, turning them frequently, until golden and toasted. Transfer to a plate and set aside.

Heat the oil in a small saucepan and add the garlic and chilli. Gently cook for 2–3 minutes until softened. Remove from the heat and set aside.

Drain the broccoli, return it to the pan and mash coarsely.

Drain the pasta and return it to the warm pan. Add the mashed broccoli, garlic and chilli oil and toasted pine nuts. Mix well, add the lemon juice and season to taste.

Divide between 2 serving plates or bowls and top with fresh Parmesan shavings. Sprinkle with black pepper and serve.

mint, ginger and almond pesto

2 cm ginger root, peeled
and grated

20 g mint leaves

8 tablespoons vegetable oil

2 tablespoons light soy sauce

1 tablespoon freshly squeezed
lime juice

1 garlic clove, crushed

100 g almonds, toasted

MAKES APPROXIMATELY 150 ML

Toasting the almonds gives the pesto a more intense flavour. Packets of pre-toasted almonds are sometimes available to buy or you can toast them yourself in the oven for 5–6 minutes at 200ºC (400ºF) Gas 6. Keep an eye on them as they burn quickly.

Put all the ingredients in the bowl of a food processor and whizz until smooth.

coriander, chilli and peanut pesto

100 g roasted and salted peanuts

1 garlic clove, crushed

1 red or green chilli, deseeded
and chopped

20 g coriander leaves

finely grated zest of 1 lime

100 ml groundnut or sunflower oil

sea salt and freshly ground
black pepper

MAKES APPROXIMATELY 150 ML

This hot and spicy pesto is perfect stirred through hot or cold pasta.

Put the peanuts, garlic and chilli in the bowl of a food processor. Blend, then add the coriander leaves and lime zest, season generously and pulse to form a coarse mix. Allow the motor to run and then, in a steady flow, add the groundnut oil to form a smooth paste. Taste and season as necessary.

red pepper and walnut pesto

2 chargrilled red peppers

55 g walnut pieces, toasted

3 spring onions, chopped

1 garlic clove, crushed

2 tablespoons chopped parsley

4–5 tablespoons extra virgin olive oil

sea salt and freshly ground
black pepper

MAKES APPROXIMATELY 150 ML

Further proof that pine nuts aren't the only type of nut that can make a fine pesto.

Put all the ingredients in a food processor and whizz until smooth. Taste and season as necessary.

Variation If you have time, roast your own red peppers; place under a preheated high grill until the skins are blackened on all sides. Put in a plastic bag for 10 minutes, then slip off the skins.

artichoke and almond pesto

4–6 roasted and marinated artichoke hearts, drained

100 g almonds, toasted

2 tablespoons chopped basil

1 garlic clove, crushed

4 tablespoons extra virgin olive oil

30 g Parmesan cheese, freshly
and finely grated

sea salt and freshly ground
black pepper

MAKES APPROXIMATELY 150 ML

This has a lovely creamy texture and subtle flavour for adding to pasta.

Put the artichokes, almonds, basil and garlic in a food processor. Blend until you have a coarse mixture. Add the oil in a thin stream with the motor running to form a smooth paste. Transfer the purée to a bowl and stir in the Parmesan cheese. Season to taste.

tagliatelle with peas and goats' cheese pesto

Crumbly goats' cheese works surprisingly well in pesto, adding a slightly creamy edge to it. Roughly crumble it in so you get pockets of the molten cheese tucked in among your tangle of tagliatelle.

1 small garlic clove, peeled but left whole

2 large green chillies, deseeded

40 g basil leaves, plus extra to serve

25 g pine nuts

100 ml extra virgin olive oil

100 g goats' cheese

250 g fresh or frozen peas

400 g dried tagliatelle

freshly grated Parmesan cheese, to serve

sea salt and freshly ground black pepper

SERVES 4

Put the garlic, chillies, basil and a large pinch of salt in a food processor and process until roughly chopped. Alternatively, crush everything with a pestle and mortar.

Put the pine nuts in a dry frying pan and toast over low heat for a few minutes, shaking the pan, until they are golden all over. Add the pine nuts to the mixture in the food processor (or the mortar) and process again until coarsely chopped. Add half the olive oil then blend again. Add the remaining oil, crumble in the goats' cheese and stir. Taste and season.

Bring a large saucepan of salted water and a small pan of unsalted water to the boil. Add the peas to the smaller pan and simmer for 4–5 minutes if fresh or 3 minutes if frozen. Once the water in the large pan comes to a rolling boil, add the pasta and cook until it is al dente or according to the instructions on the packet. Drain and tip back into the pan.

Add 2–3 good dollops of pesto and the peas to the tagliatelle and toss through the hot strands, then add the remaining pesto making sure all the pasta is thoroughly coated. Transfer to bowls and sprinkle with basil and freshly grated Parmesan.

cheese and cream

basic cream sauce with butter and parmesan

250 g egg-based dried pasta or
1 packet stuffed fresh pasta

250 ml single cream

25 g unsalted butter

3 tablespoons freshly grated
Parmesan cheese, plus extra for
serving

lots of freshly ground black pepper
or freshly grated nutmeg

3 tablespoons finely chopped herbs,
such as parsley, fennel, coriander
or basil (optional)

grated zest of ½ unwaxed
lemon (optional)

SERVES 4

This basic sauce provides the departure point for a variety of other sauces. Stir in some cooked poultry, fish or vegetables as a feast for unexpected guests. Add herbs, nuts or cheese to make a delicious sauce for stuffed pasta. Always dress the pasta in a bowl rather than the pan, because the heat of the pan will dry out dairy-based sauces.

Bring a large saucepan of salted water to the boil. Add the pasta and cook until al dente, or according to the instructions on the packet. Drain well, reserving 100ml of the cooking water. Return the pasta to the pan to keep warm.

Put the cream and butter in a shallow saucepan over low heat. Bring to simmering point, shaking the pan from time to time. Leave to simmer for a few minutes or until the sauce starts to thicken. Add the Parmesan and pepper or nutmeg and stir.

Stir the sauce and half of the cooking water into the pasta. Mix until well coated. Add extra water if necessary and stir again. Serve at once with extra Parmesan, herbs and lemon zest, if using.

Variation Add 100 g thinly sliced smoked salmon or trout and 3 tablespoons finely chopped dill or fennel to the pasta at the same time as the cream sauce, and stir gently.

spaghetti alla carbonara

7 oz dried pasta, such as spaghetti, tagliatelle or linguine

1 tablespoon butter

1 shallot, finely chopped

2 garlic cloves, finely chopped

6 slices bacon, chopped

2 medium eggs

150 ml single cream

2 tablespoons freshly grated Parmesan cheese, plus extra to serve

sea salt and freshly ground black pepper

SERVES 2

This dish is ready to eat in the time it takes the pasta to cook. It's traditionally served with spaghetti, but tagliatelle or linguine work too.

Cook the pasta in salted, boiling water until al dente or according to the timings on the packet.

Meanwhile, heat the butter in a small frying pan, add the shallot, garlic and bacon and cook for 5 minutes until golden. Put the eggs, cream and Parmesan into a bowl and beat, adding salt and pepper to taste.

Drain the pasta and return it to the warm pan. Remove from the heat and add the shallot mixture. Add the egg mixture and toss well to coat. Serve topped with Parmesan and black pepper.

creamy vodka sauce

250 g dried pasta, such as fusilli or fusilli bucati

1 tablespoon butter

2 plum tomatoes, coarsely chopped

1 garlic clove, finely chopped

4 tablespoons chilli vodka

150 ml double cream

sea salt and freshly ground black pepper

a few chives, halved, to serve

freshly grated Parmesan cheese

SERVES 2

If you don't have chilli vodka, add a small, finely chopped chilli at the same time as the garlic and use ordinary vodka instead.

Cook the pasta in salted, boiling water until al dente or according to the timings on the packet.

Meanwhile, heat the butter in a small saucepan, add the tomatoes and garlic and cook for 3 minutes. Add the vodka and boil rapidly for 2 minutes. Reduce the heat and simmer for 2–3 minutes, then stir in the cream and simmer gently for a further 5 minutes. Add salt and pepper to taste.

Drain the pasta and return it to the warm pan. Add the sauce and mix well. Serve topped with Parmesan, chives and pepper.

parma ham, rocket and bubbling blue cheese

300 g dried pasta, such as
pappardelle or lasagnette

2 tablespoons olive oil

8 slices Parma ham

250 g cherry tomatoes

2 Bleu de Bresse or mini Cambozola
cheeses, 150 g each

2 tablespoons Marsala or sherry

2 tablespoons chopped
flat leaf parsley

a handful of rocket

sea salt and freshly ground
black pepper

SERVES 4

The Parma ham crisps up beautifully in a non-stick frying pan – other cured hams can also be used, such as serrano, San Daniele or speck.

Bring a large saucepan of salted water to the boil. Add the pasta and cook until al dente, or according to the packet instructions.

Heat a little of the oil in a frying pan, add the Parma ham and cook for 1 minute on each side until crisp. Remove and drain on kitchen paper. Add the remaining oil to the pan. When hot, add the cherry tomatoes and cook for 3–4 minutes until split and softened.

Meanwhile, cut each cheese in half crossways, put cut side up under an overhead grill and cook for 2–3 minutes, until golden and bubbling.

Break the Parma ham into pieces and add to the tomato pan. Add the Marsala or sherry, parsley and salt and pepper to taste.

Drain the pasta well and return it to the warm pan. Add the Parma ham and tomato mixture and toss gently to mix. Divide between 4 serving plates or bowls and sprinkle with rocket. Using a spatula, slide a bubbling cheese half on top of each. Sprinkle with black pepper and serve immediately.

béchamel sauce with prosciutto, emmental and salad leaves

500 g dried farfalle or ridged penne

50 g unsalted butter

25 g plain flour

250 ml warm milk

1 small onion, finely chopped

200 g iceberg lettuce, shredded

½ nutmeg, freshly grated, plus extra to taste

125 g prosciutto, sliced into thin strips

sea salt and freshly ground black pepper

60 g Emmental cheese shavings

freshly grated Parmesan cheese

SERVES 4–6

Prosciutto and salad never tasted as good as in this simple supper dish. Finely shredded Savoy cabbage, leeks or bok choy can be used instead of iceberg lettuce. Vegetarians might like to add 125 g chopped walnuts instead of ham.

Bring a large saucepan of salted water to the boil. Add the pasta and cook until al dente, or according to the packet instructions.

To make the béchamel sauce, put 25 g butter in a saucepan and melt until it starts to bubble. Add the flour and mix well. Cook over gentle heat for 1–2 minutes, add the milk and continue cooking until the sauce thickens. Stir constantly with a wire whisk to stop lumps forming. Add salt and nutmeg to taste.

To cook the vegetables, gently melt the remaining butter in a large frying pan. Add the onion and fry over low heat until transparent. Add the lettuce and continue cooking for 5 minutes. Sprinkle the nutmeg onto the lettuce and onion as they are cooking. When the lettuce has wilted, add the prosciutto and béchamel sauce and stir. Add salt and pepper to taste.

Add the sauce to the drained pasta and mix until well coated. Sprinkle Emmental shavings over the top and serve grated Parmesan alongside the dish.

Variation Instead of lettuce, use 500 g mushrooms sautéed in butter with thyme and garlic, add to the béchamel sauce and serve with Parmesan shavings.

tagliatelle with broccoli, anchovies, parmesan and crème fraîche

175 g dried tagliatelle

300 g broccoli florets

1 tablespoon olive oil

2 garlic cloves, crushed

½ teaspoon dried chilli flakes

3 anchovy fillets, roughly chopped

100 g crème fraîche

sea salt and freshly ground black pepper

freshly grated Parmesan cheese, to serve

SERVES 2

You can save time and washing up here by cooking the broccoli in the same pan as the pasta. If it's in season, use purple sprouting broccoli. The anchovies are already very salty, so it's best to taste a forkful before adding any more salt.

Bring a large saucepan of salted water to the boil. Add the pasta and cook until al dente, or according to the packet instructions. Add the broccoli to the pasta 3–4 minutes before the end of cooking. Drain the pasta and the broccoli well and reserve around 4 tablespoons of the cooking water.

Wipe out the pan and add the oil. Cook the garlic, chilli flakes and anchovies over low heat for about 2 minutes. Add the crème fraîche, season with a little pepper and bring to the boil. Return the cooked broccoli and pasta to the pan, adding a little of the reserved cooking water if necessary to thin the sauce down. Season to taste with black pepper.

Divide the pasta between serving bowls and serve immediately, sprinkled with Parmesan cheese.

This simple recipe is ideal for family meals or any unexpected guests. The combination of creamy mascarpone and salty pancetta is hard to beat.

penne with mascarpone, spinach and pancetta

150 g pancetta, diced

1 garlic clove, finely chopped

500 g dried penne

200 g mascarpone cheese

50 g Parmesan cheese, grated, plus extra to serve

200 g young spinach leaves, washed and dried

sea salt and freshly ground black pepper

SERVES 4

Heat a large frying pan over medium heat for a few minutes. Add the pancetta and garlic and cook until the fat runs and the pancetta is crispy and golden.

Bring a large saucepan of salted water to the boil. Add the pasta and cook until al dente or according to the instructions on the packet. Drain, reserving 4 tablespoons of the cooking water, and return to the saucepan.

Meanwhile, put the mascarpone in a small saucepan, add the reserved water and heat through gently. Add to the pasta with the Parmesan and a generous grinding of black pepper, and stir well.

Add the spinach and garlic and pancetta, including the fat from the frying pan, and stir well. Serve immediately with Parmesan.

Variation Instead of spinach, try rocket or lightly cooked leeks, peas, broad beans, French beans or carrots.

gorgonzola, pecan and mascarpone sauce

25 g unsalted butter

1 garlic clove, crushed

175 g Gorgonzola cheese, crumbled

175 g mascarpone cheese

a pinch of ground mace or a little freshly grated nutmeg

100 g pecan nuts, toasted and roughly chopped

2 tablespoons snipped fresh chives

sea salt and freshly ground black pepper

SERVES 4

The toasted pecan nuts add texture to this rich and creamy cheese sauce. Gorgonzola is a strongly flavoured blue cheese that is perfect combined with the milder mascarpone. Other blue cheeses you could use are Roquefort or even Stilton.

Melt the butter in a saucepan. Add the garlic and gently fry over low heat for 2–3 minutes. Stir in the Gorgonzola, mascarpone, mace and a little seasoning. Cook gently until the sauce is heated through but the cheese still has a little texture.

Remove the pan from the heat and stir in the pecan nuts and chives. Season to taste and serve hot.

mushroom cream sauce with garlic, parsley and marsala

50 g unsalted butter

1 garlic clove, crushed

1 tablespoon chopped parsley, plus extra to serve

250 g closed mushrooms, thinly sliced

40 ml Marsala wine or sherry

125 ml vegetable or chicken stock

250 ml single cream

250 g dried pasta, such as pappardelle, tagliatelle, fettucine or farfalle

3 tablespoons freshly grated Parmesan cheese, plus extra to serve

sea salt and freshly ground black pepper

SERVES 4

Keep a bottle of Marsala in the cupboard for cooking – it has a very distinctive flavour and is useful for both sweet and savoury dishes. It is used frequently in Bolognese cooking, and in Sicily from where it hails originally. This sauce also goes equally well with pan-fried steak, veal and pork.

Melt the butter in a frying pan. Add the garlic, parsley and mushrooms and cook gently over low heat, stirring from time to time. When the mushrooms have reduced and are starting to soften, add the Marsala and salt and pepper to taste. Stir well, cover the pan with a lid and leave to cook for a further 30 minutes, adding a little stock now and then. The mushrooms should be moist, but not watery. Add the cream and heat gently, shaking the pan occasionally.

Towards the end of the cooking time, bring a large saucepan of salted water to the boil. Add the pasta and cook until al dente, or according to the packet instructions. Drain well.

Add the sauce and the Parmesan to the freshly cooked pasta. Divide between 4 serving plates or bowls, sprinkle with the extra chopped parsley and serve at once with extra Parmesan.

Variation Cook small cubes of aubergine instead of mushrooms.

asparagus tagliatelle

250 ml single cream

300 g dried tagliatelle pasta or similiar

1 bunch of fine asparagus, trimmed and each spear cut into 4

grated zest and freshly squeezed juice of 1 unwaxed lemon

3 tablespoons finely chopped flat leaf parsley

100 g finely grated Parmesan cheese

sea salt and freshly ground black pepper

SERVES 4, AS A STARTER

Young asparagus is one of life's great gifts, but don't miss its rather short seasonal window, especially the British asparagus season which really kicks off in May and ends in June. This is a perfect pasta starter, combining the prime spears with a handful of other fresh, good-quality ingredients.

Put the cream in a small saucepan and bring to the boil. Reduce the heat to a low simmer and cook for 8–10 minutes, until slightly thickened. Set aside.

Bring a large saucepan of salted water to the boil. Add the pasta and cook until al dente, or according to the packet instructions. About 2 minutes before the pasta is cooked, add the asparagus to the boiling water. Drain well and return to the warm pan with the reduced cream, lemon zest and juice, parsley and half of the Parmesan. Toss together, season well with salt and pepper and serve with the remaining cheese sprinkled on top.

Variation As a substitute to asparagus, pan-fry 1 grated courgette in 1 tablespoon butter over medium heat until softened and golden. Add the courgette to the well-drained pasta along with the other ingredients.

pasta with courgette, mint, lemon and cream

This makes a deliciously summery dish. You can make it with either green or yellow courgettes (the smaller, the better), or you could use little pattypan summer squashes. You could also toss some shredded golden yellow courgette flowers in at the very last moment to barely wilt in the heat of the pasta.

40 g unsalted butter

300–350 g small courgettes, topped, tailed and cut into chunky matchsticks

200 g dried pasta of your choice

125 ml dry vermouth (optional)

150 ml double cream or crème fraîche

finely grated zest of 1 large unwaxed lemon

freshly squeezed lemon juice, to taste

2 tablespoons chopped mint

3–4 tablespoons toasted pine nuts

a few courgette flowers, to serve (optional)

sea salt and freshly ground black pepper

SERVES 2

Melt the butter in a frying pan over low heat and add the courgettes and a pinch of salt. Cook gently for about 10 minutes until tender but barely browned.

Meanwhile, bring a large saucepan of salted water to the boil and cook the pasta until al dente or according to the packet instructions. Drain, reserving a little of the cooking water.

Turn up the heat under the courgettes and add the vermouth (if using) or 4–5 tablespoons of the cooking water and let it bubble and evaporate. Add the cream and lemon zest, and again let it bubble, reduce and thicken slightly. If it reduces too much, add another 1–2 tablespoons cooking water. Add a squeeze or two of lemon juice as necessary and toss with the pasta and mint.

Serve immediately with a grinding of pepper and a sprinkling of toasted pine nuts.

lemon and vermouth sauce

This is quite an unusual sauce for pasta, but no less wonderful for it. If you cannot find unwaxed lemons, be sure to wash the skins well before grating the zest.

400–500 g dried pasta of your choice

finely grated zest of 2 unwaxed lemons

125 ml dry vermouth

200 ml double cream

50 g Parmesan cheese, freshly grated, plus extra to serve

2 tablespoons chopped basil

sea salt and freshly ground black pepper

SERVES 4

Bring a large saucepan of salted water to the boil. Add the pasta and cook until al dente, or according to the packet instructions.

Put the lemon zest and vermouth in a small saucepan, bring to the boil, then simmer until the liquid is reduced by half. Leave to cool for 5 minutes.

Beat in the cream and return to the heat until warmed through. Stir in the Parmesan and basil and season to taste. Serve at once, sprinkled with extra grated Parmesan.

tagliolini with lemon and green olives

125 g unsalted butter

finely grated zest of 2 unwaxed lemons

125 g green olives, chopped

1 tablespoon chopped lemon thyme (optional)

250 g dried pasta such as egg tagliolini, paglia e fieno or linguine

50 g grated Parmesan or pecorino cheese, plus extra to serve

sea salt and freshly ground black pepper

SERVES 4 AS A STARTER OR 2 AS A MAIN COURSE

You couldn't find a simpler pasta dish to prepare. It makes a very elegant starter when served in small portions, or a filling main course. Try to keep the butter melted for as long as possible so the lemon oil is fully infused.

Melt the butter slowly in a stainless steel or non-reactive pan and add the lemon zest. Leave over a very gentle heat or in a warm place to infuse for at least 2 hours (or for as long as you have), remelting if necessary.

When ready to eat, strain the melted butter (reheat if necessary), then add the chopped olives, lemon thyme, if using, and salt and pepper to taste. Keep it warm.

Bring a large saucepan of salted water to the boil. Add the pasta and cook until al dente, or according to the packet instructions. Drain, reserving 2–3 tablespoons of the cooking water. Toss the pasta with the lemon and olive butter, Parmesan, more pepper if you like, and some of the reserved cooking water if it looks too dry. Serve with extra Parmesan.

Variations
• Add lots of cracked black pepper to the strained lemon butter. Omit the olives and add 75 g chopped rocket leaves and plenty of grated Parmesan.

• Instead of the lemon zest, infuse bay leaves in the butter and add 250 g halved cherry tomatoes.

fusilli with salsa verde and chargrilled cheese

300 g dried pasta, such as fusilli

2 anchovy fillets in oil, drained

1 tablespoon capers

1 green chilli, deseeded and
finely chopped

1 garlic clove, crushed

3 tablespoons chopped
flat leaf parsley

1 tablespoon chopped coriander

2 teaspoons Dijon mustard

4 tablespoons olive oil

1 tablespoon white wine vinegar

2 tablespoons plain flour

250 g halloumi or provolone cheese,
cut into 1-cm-thick slices

1 teaspoon freshly ground
black pepper

SERVES 4

The salsa verde can vary according to the herbs you have to hand – parsley should always be the base, but feel free to add basil, tarragon or mint instead of the coriander.

Bring a large saucepan of salted water to the boil. Add the pasta and cook until al dente, or according to the packet instructions.

Meanwhile, to make the salsa verde, put the anchovy fillets and capers onto a chopping board and, using a heavy knife, chop finely. Put the chilli and garlic on top and chop again until very finely chopped. Transfer to a bowl and add the herbs, mustard, 3 tablespoons of the oil and the vinegar.

Heat the remaining oil in a stove-top grill pan until hot. Put the flour onto a small plate, add the black pepper and mix. Dip each cheese slice in the flour to coat on both sides, shaking off any excess. Cook in the grill pan for 1–2 minutes on each side until golden brown, then remove and drain on kitchen paper.

Drain the pasta well and return it to the warm pan. Add the salsa verde and toss to mix. Divide between 4 serving plates or bowls, arrange the cheese on top and serve immediately.

roasted pumpkin with sage, lemon and mozzarella butter

2 tablespoons olive oil

500 g pumpkin or butternut squash

1 teaspoon cumin seeds

150 g mozzarella cheese, drained and coarsely chopped

50 g butter, softened

2 garlic cloves, crushed

2 teaspoons chopped sage leaves, plus extra whole leaves, to serve

grated zest and juice of 1 unwaxed lemon

300 g dried pasta, such as fusilli bucati or cavatappi

sea salt and freshly ground black pepper

SERVES 4

Tantalizing pockets of melting garlic butter flavoured with herbs and cheese complement the succulent chunks of roast pumpkin in this tasty autumnal dish.

Preheat the oven to 200°C (400F°) Gas 6.

Put the oil in a roasting tin and transfer to the oven for 5 minutes, until hot.

Using a small, sharp knife, peel the pumpkin or butternut, remove the seeds and cut the flesh into cubes, about 2.5 cm.

Add the cumin seeds to the hot oil in the roasting tin, then add the pumpkin and salt and pepper to taste. Toss to coat. Roast in the oven for 30 minutes, turning the pumpkin from time to time until tender and golden brown.

Put the mozzarella, butter, garlic, sage, lemon zest and juice and salt and pepper to taste into a food processor. Blend to a coarse paste. Transfer to a sheet of greaseproof paper and roll into a cylinder. Chill for at least 20 minutes or until firm enough to slice.

Meanwhile, bring a large saucepan of salted water to the boil. Add the pasta and cook until al dente, or according to the instructions on the packet.

Drain the pasta and return it to the warm pan. Add the roasted pumpkin. Slice or dice the mozzarella butter and add to the pasta. Toss, divide between 4 serving plates or bowls, top with sage leaves and serve immediately.

penne with mozzarella and tomatoes

400 g dried penne rigate

400 g tinn chopped plum tomatoes

1 small dried red chilli

3–4 garlic cloves, chopped

1 onion, chopped

2 tablespoons tomato paste or purée

leaves from 2 sprigs of oregano, marjoram, basil or rosemary, chopped or torn

1 tablespoon sugar

1 tablespoon balsamic vinegar (optional)

50 g capers, or black olives (optional)

150 g mozzarella cheese, sliced thinly or torn into shreds

sea salt and freshly ground black pepper

2 tablespoons extra virgin olive oil, to serve

sprigs of basil, to serve

SERVES 4

In Italy, pasta tends to be served as a starter – as a course in itself, after the appetizer or antipasto but before the main dish. Make sure the temperatures are right: the cheese must melt and trickle.

Bring a large saucepan of salted water to the boil. Add the pasta and cook until al dente, or according to the packet instructions.

Meanwhile, to make the sauce, put the tomatoes in a large, shallow saucepan or frying pan. Add the chilli, garlic, onion, tomato paste, oregano, sugar, and if using, the balsamic vinegar and capers. Cook, stirring, over high heat until the sauce is thick and reduced to about half its original volume. Add salt and pepper to taste.

Drain the pasta, reserving 3 tablespoons of the cooking water, then return the pasta and reserved water to the saucepan. Add the sliced mozzarella. Pour the hot sauce over the top and toss and stir until well mixed and the mozzarella is softened and melting. Sprinkle with the oil and serve topped with sprigs of basil.

slow-roasted tomatoes with ricotta and spaghetti

6 large, ripe tomatoes

4 sprigs of oregano, plus
2 tablespoons chopped oregano

7 tablespoons extra virgin olive oil

500 g dried spaghetti

4 garlic cloves, sliced

1 dried red chilli, chopped

freshly squeezed juice of ½ lemon

200 g ricotta cheese,
crumbled into big pieces

sea salt and freshly ground
black pepper

freshly grated Parmesan, to serve

SERVES 4

A pasta dish packed full of the flavours of the Mediterranean – garlic, tomatoes, oregano and ricotta. Roast the tomatoes ahead of time if you like and then reheat at 180°C (350°F) Gas 4 for 15 minutes.

Preheat the oven to 250°C (500°F) Gas 9.

Cut the tomatoes in half and arrange, cut side up, in a shallow roasting tin. Sprinkle with the sprigs of oregano, 1 tablespoon of the oil and lots of salt and pepper.

Roast in a preheated oven for 20 minutes. Reduce to 150°C (300°F) Gas 2 and cook for a further 1–1½ hours until the tomatoes are golden, glossy and reduced in size by about one-third. Remove from the oven and keep them warm.

Bring a large saucepan of salted water to the boil. Add the pasta and cook until al dente, or according to the packet instructions.

After about 5 minutes, put the remaining oil into a large, deep frying pan, heat well, add the garlic and fry gently for 2 minutes. Add the chilli and cook for a further minute.

Drain the cooked pasta, reserving 4 tablespoons of the cooking water. Add the pasta and the reserved cooking water to the frying pan, then add the chopped oregano, lemon juice and salt and pepper. Toss over the heat for about 2 minutes.

Divide between 4 serving plates or bowls and serve topped with the tomatoes and ricotta and a light dusting of Parmesan.

penne with melted ricotta and herby parmesan sauce

350 g dried penne or other pasta

6 tablespoons extra virgin olive oil

100 g pine nuts

125 g rocket leaves, chopped

2 tablespoons chopped parsley

2 tablespoons chopped basil

250 g ricotta cheese, mashed

50 g freshly grated Parmesan cheese

sea salt and freshly ground
black pepper

SERVES 4

Pasta is the archetypal fast food. This dish is fast and fresh, with the ricotta melting into the hot pasta and coating it like a creamy sauce. The pine nuts give it crunch, while the herbs lend a fresh, scented flavour.

Bring a large saucepan of salted water to the boil. Add the pasta and cook until al dente, or according to the packet instructions.

Meanwhile, heat the oil in a frying pan, add the pine nuts and fry gently until golden. Set aside.

Drain the cooked pasta, reserving 4 tablespoons of the cooking water, and return both to the pan. Add the pine nuts and their oil, the herbs, ricotta, half the Parmesan and season to taste. Stir until evenly coated with the sauce.

Divide between 4 serving plates or bowls and serve immediately with the remaining Parmesan sprinkled on top.

A delicate and original starter for a party, this is more a dressing than a sauce because there is no cooking involved. It can be prepared in the time it takes to cook the pasta. The combination of savoury and sweet elements such as cheese and sweet spices dates back to Roman times.

ricotta, cinnamon and walnut sauce

500 g dried pasta, such as spaghettini, linguine or rigatoni

250 g ricotta cheese

75 g unsalted butter, softened

1 teaspoon icing sugar

1 teaspoon ground cinnamon or mixed spice

5 tablespoons chopped walnuts, plus 1½ tablespoons chopped walnuts, to serve

sea salt and freshly ground black pepper

freshly grated Parmesan cheese, to serve

SERVES 4–6

Bring a large saucepan of salted water to the boil. Add the pasta and cook until al dente, or according to the instructions on the packet. Drain well, reserving 100 ml of the cooking water and return to the pan.

Put the ricotta, butter, icing sugar and cinnamon in a bowl and beat with a wooden spoon until smooth and creamy. Add salt and pepper to taste and stir in half the reserved cooking water.

Add the ricotta mixture to the pasta, add the remaining cooking water if needed to improve the consistency, then stir in the 5 tablespoons walnuts. Mix well until coated. Serve at once, topped with the extra walnuts and Parmesan.

Variation Try toasted pine nuts or almonds instead of walnuts.

pasta bakes

600 ml passata

150 ml red wine

1 teaspoon brown sugar

1 garlic clove, crushed

1 bay leaf

1 tablespoon olive oil

12 dried cannelloni tubes

parsley and pancetta filling

2 tablespoons olive oil

1 onion, finely chopped

2 garlic cloves, finely chopped

125 g cubed pancetta

4 tablespoons chopped
flat leaf parsley

200 g fresh white breadcrumbs

150 ml double cream

grated zest and juice of 1 unwaxed
lemon

150 g mozzarella cheese, drained
and cubed

sea salt and freshly ground
black pepper

a baking dish, about 30 x 20 cm

SERVES 4

parsley and pancetta cannelloni

It is best not to precook the cannelloni tubes, as this makes them difficult to stuff. So to compensate for the moisture they will absorb as they cook, the sauce should be runny – it will become thicker and rich.

Put the passata, wine, sugar, garlic, bay leaf and oil into a saucepan. Add salt and pepper to taste and bring to the boil. Cover with a lid and simmer for 15 minutes.

Preheat the oven to 190°C (375°F) Gas 5.

To make the filling, heat 1 tablespoon of the oil in a saucepan, add the onion, garlic and pancetta and cook for 4–5 minutes until softened and golden. Add the parsley, breadcrumbs, cream, lemon zest and juice and salt and pepper to taste.

Spoon the filling mixture into the cannelloni tubes and arrange the stuffed tubes in the baking dish. Pour the tomato sauce over the top and sprinkle with the mozzarella. Bake in the preheated oven for 40 minutes, or until the top is bubbling and golden and the pasta is cooked through.

250 g cherry tomatoes

1 red onion, finely chopped

2 garlic cloves, finely chopped

2 tablespoons olive oil

300 g dried small macaroni

4 boneless, skinless chicken thighs, quartered crossways

200 g chorizo sausage, thickly sliced

2 teaspoons chopped rosemary

1 litre chicken stock

a pinch of saffron threads

8 large, uncooked prawns

sea salt and freshly ground black pepper

a handful of basil leaves, torn, to serve

a heavy roasting tin

SERVES 4

oven-roasted spicy macaroni

Inspired by paella, this is absolutely delicious, and never fails to impress and delight. It's all cooked in the oven, so really couldn't be easier.

Preheat the oven to 220°C (400°F) Gas 7.

Put the cherry tomatoes into the roasting tin and sprinkle with the red onion, garlic and oil. Roast in the preheated oven for 20 minutes until the tomatoes are soft.

Remove from the oven and add the macaroni, chicken, chorizo, rosemary, stock, saffron and salt and pepper to taste. Mix well and return to the oven to bake for 30 minutes.

Add the prawns and bake for a further 5 minutes until the pasta and chicken are cooked. Sprinkle with basil and serve.

classic lasagne

500 g dried lasagne

1 litre milk

1 small garlic clove, peeled but
left whole

50 g butter

50 g plain flour

1 quantity Classic Bolognese Sauce
(page 45)

300 g mozzarella cheese, drained
and diced

4 tablespoons freshly grated
Parmesan cheese

sea salt and freshly ground
black pepper

a baking dish, about 30 x 20 cm

SERVES 8

It is best to take the time to boil the lasagne first –
if not, the pasta tends to draw moisture from the
sauce as it cooks, and the finished dish can be dry.

Preheat the oven to 190°C (375°F) Gas 5.

Bring a large saucepan of salted water to the boil. Add the lasagne
sheets, one at a time so that they don't stick together. Cook for 5
minutes, then drain and tip the lasagne into a bowl of cold water.
Drain again and pat dry with kitchen paper.

To make the white sauce, put the milk and garlic into a small
saucepan and heat gently until warm. Melt the butter in a separate
saucepan, then stir in the flour and cook for 1 minute. Gradually
add the warm milk, stirring constantly to make a smooth sauce.
Bring to the boil, then simmer for 2–3 minutes. Remove and
discard the garlic clove. Add salt and pepper to taste.

Put 3–4 tablespoons of the Classic Bolognese Sauce into the
baking dish, spread evenly across the base of the dish and cover
with a layer of lasagne. Spoon over some white sauce and a few
pieces of mozzarella and continue adding layers, starting with
another layer of bolognese sauce and finishing with the white
sauce and mozzarella, until all the ingredients have been used.
Sprinkle with black pepper and Parmesan, then bake in the
preheated oven for 30 minutes until the top is crusty and golden.

pot luck summer pasta

500 g dried penne or rigatoni

2 tablespoons olive oil

800 g tinned plum tomatoes, drained and deseeded

6 garlic cloves, lightly crushed

1 teaspoon dried oregano or 1 small piece of chilli, to taste

150 g cooked peas, sweetcorn or sliced mushrooms

370 g tinned tuna in oil, half drained

1 tablespoon capers

100 g cooked ham or chicken, cut into slivers

150 g mozzarella cheese, diced

50 g salami, finely chopped (optional)

15 g crisp breadcrumbs*

extra virgin olive oil, for frying and drizzling

béchamel sauce

40 g butter

40 g flour

400 ml warmed milk

freshly grated nutmeg

sea salt and freshly ground black pepper

a baking dish, about 30 x 20 cm

SERVES 4

This dish is extremely versatile, meaning that you can vary the type and quantities of vegetables, meat and fish to suit your taste and what you have to hand.

Preheat the oven to 220°C (425°F) Gas 7.

Bring a large saucepan of salted water to the boil, add the pasta and cook until slightly less than al dente. Drain, reserving 2 tablespoons of the cooking water, and return to the pan.

Meanwhile, heat the oil in a medium saucepan over high heat. When the oil is searing hot, add the tomatoes. Cook for 1–2 minutes, taking care not to burn the tomatoes, but allowing them to caramelize a little. Reduce the heat and mash the tomatoes with a potato masher, then add the garlic and oregano. Stir well, cover and cook for a few minutes, then add the mushrooms, if using, cover and cook for 20 minutes. Stir in the tuna, capers, peas and ham and heat through.

To make the béchamel sauce melt the butter in a small saucepan. When it starts to bubble, add the flour and mix well. Cook over gentle heat for 1–2 minutes, then whisk in the milk and continue cooking until the sauce thickens. Add grated nutmeg and season to taste.

Add the tomato sauce to the pasta with the reserved water and mix until the pasta is well coated. Stir in the mozzarella and salami, if using. Transfer to a large, shallow, buttered ovenproof dish and pour the béchamel sauce over the top. Sprinkle with the breadcrumbs. Drizzle with olive oil and bake in the preheated oven for 20–30 minutes until golden. Serve immediately.

*Note To make crisp breadcrumbs, cut the crusts off a large, slightly stale, white loaf and lay them on a large baking sheet. Bake in a preheated oven at 100°C (200°F) Gas ½ for about 1 hour until they have dried out completely and are crisp all the way through. Leave to cool, break into large pieces, then put in a food processor and reduce to fine crumbs.

three cheese
baked penne

350 g dried penne

400 g mascarpone cheese

2 tablespoons wholegrain mustard

300 g Fontina cheese, grated

4 tablespoons freshly grated
Parmesan cheese

sea salt and freshly ground
black pepper

a baking dish, about 30 x 20 cm

SERVES 4

This is a simplified version of that old-time favourite, macaroni cheese. The recipe calls for mascarpone rather than white sauce so there is no risk of lumps.

Preheat the oven to 200°C (400°F) Gas 6.

Bring a large saucepan of salted water to the boil. Add the pasta, and cook until al dente, or according to the packet instructions.

Drain the pasta well and return it to the warm pan. Add the mascarpone and stir to mix. Add the mustard, Fontina and Parmesan, with salt and pepper to taste. Stir to mix.

Transfer to the baking dish and cook in the preheated oven for 25–30 minutes until golden and bubbling.

ricotta, basil and cherry tomato cannelloni

This can all be assembled the day before, refrigerated and put in the oven at the last moment. You can vary the type of cheese, as long as it is a soft one.

750 g ripe cherry tomatoes, whole

5 tablespoons good olive oil

2 teaspoons dried oregano

2 teaspoons sugar

300 g ricotta cheese

6 tablespoons fresh red or green pesto

12 fresh lasagne sheets

350 g vine-ripened tomatoes, thinly sliced (you need 24 slices)

3 tablespoons freshly grated Parmesan cheese

a handful of basil leaves, to serve

green salad, to serve

sea salt and freshly ground black pepper

a baking dish, about 20 x 25 cm

SERVES 4

Preheat the oven to 220°C (425°F) Gas 7.

Cut 250 g of the whole cherry tomatoes in half and set aside for the top.

Heat the oil in a frying pan, add the uncut tomatoes (they will splutter a little) and cover tightly. Cook over high heat, shaking the pan occasionally, for 5 minutes until the tomatoes start to break down. Uncover and stir in the oregano and sugar and salt and pepper to taste. Set aside.

Soften the cheese in a bowl and beat in the pesto. Put all the sheets of lasagne on a work surface and spread the cheese mixture evenly over them. Put 2 tomato slices on each sheet, season well and roll up from the narrow side like a Swiss roll. Spoon half the tomato sauce in the bottom of the baking dish. Put the pasta rolls on top of the sauce, then spoon over the remaining sauce. Dot with the reserved cherry tomato halves and cover with foil.

Bake in the preheated oven for 25–30 minutes. Uncover, sprinkle with the Parmesan and grill for a further 10 minutes until beginning to brown. Remove from the oven and leave to stand for 10 minutes.

Top with the basil and serve with a crisp green salad.

Note If using dried lasagne sheets, cook in boiling salted water according to the packet instructions. Carefully lift them out of the water and drain through a colander. Transfer to a bowl of cold water. Drain each sheet before spreading with the cheese mixture.

macaroni, spinach and cheese bake

250 g dried macaroni

50 g unsalted butter

50 g plain flour

500 ml milk

150 g cooked spinach, well drained

200 g Parmesan cheese, freshly grated

sea salt and freshly ground black pepper

a baking dish, about 30 x 20 cm

SERVES 4

The spinach adds some colour and vitamins to this hearty bake. Fresh or frozen spinach can be used, but do make sure that both are thoroughly drained.

Preheat the oven to 190°C (375°F) Gas 5.

Bring a large saucepan of salted water to the boil. Add the pasta, and cook until al dente, or according to the packet instructions.

Meanwhile, melt the butter in a saucepan, remove from the heat and mix in the flour to make a roux. Return to a low heat and slowly pour in the milk, stirring constantly. Bring to the boil and cook for 1 minute, stirring frequently.

Drain the macaroni and add to the sauce along with the spinach, seasoning and half the Parmesan. Mix well. Pour the mixture into the baking dish, scatter the remaining Parmesan on top and bake for 15 minutes, until golden.

wild mushroom lasagne

375-g pack fresh lasagne sheets

béchamel sauce

50 g butter

2 tablespoons plain flour

¼ teaspoon freshly grated nutmeg

750 ml milk

wild mushroom filling

50 g butter

1 tablespoon olive oil

1 large white onion, sliced

2 garlic cloves, chopped

2 bay leaves

1 kg wild mushrooms, sliced

250 ml vegetable stock

1 tablespoon tomato purée

300 g Fontina cheese, grated

50 g finely grated Parmesan cheese

sea salt and freshly ground
black pepper

a baking dish, about 30 x 20 cm

SERVES 8

Lasagne may well be one of the best-loved of all Italian pasta dishes. Here, mushrooms are combined with Fontina cheese and a creamy béchamel sauce, with mouthwatering results.

To make the béchamel sauce, put the butter in a saucepan set over medium heat. When the butter sizzles, stir in the flour and nutmeg and cook for 1 minute, stirring constantly. Remove from the heat and pour the milk into the pan, whisking constantly. Return the pan to low heat and cook for 5 minutes, stirring constantly, until the sauce is smooth and creamy.

Preheat the oven to 180°C (350°F) Gas 4.

For the wild mushroom filling, put the butter and oil in a frying pan set over high heat and add the onion, garlic and bay leaves. Cook for 5 minutes until the onion has softened and turned opaque. Add the mushrooms, reduce the heat to medium and cook for 15 minutes, stirring occasionally, until the mushrooms are evenly cooked. Add the stock and tomato purée and increase the heat to high. Simmer rapidly until the liquid has reduced by half. Season well with salt and pepper.

Line the bottom of an oiled baking dish with lasagne sheets. Spread over a quarter of the béchamel sauce. Add one-third each of the wild mushrooms and grated cheese. Repeat the process and finish with a sheet of lasagne. Spoon over the remaining sauce and sprinkle with Parmesan. Bake in the preheated oven for 45 minutes, until golden brown and bubbling. Leave to rest for 10 minutes before serving.

Do not refrigerate tomatoes! Tomatoes picked before they are fully mature will keep on ripening and they do so correctly at room temperature. This sauce should be sweet and fruity so it's the perfect dish to make use of tomatoes that have been sitting in your fruit bowl, turning all lovely, soft and very ripe. It's important to use a light olive oil here; extra virgin olive oil burns at a lower temperature and will make the aubergine bitter and oily.

baked ziti with aubergine, basil and ricotta

400 g dried ziti, or other large tube shaped pasta, such as rigatoni

185 ml light olive oil

1 aubergine, halved and cut into 0.5-cm thick slices

1 onion, chopped

2 garlic cloves, chopped

3 tomatoes, chopped

1 small handful of basil leaves, torn

125 ml red wine

125 g ricotta cheese

45 g grated pecorino cheese

sea salt and freshly ground black pepper

a baking dish, about 30 x 20 cm

SERVES 4

Preheat the oven to 220°C (425°F) Gas 7.

Bring a large saucepan of salted water to the boil. Add the pasta, and cook until al dente, or according to the packet instructions. Drain well and return to the warm pan.

Heat the oil in a frying pan and when it is hot, but not smoking, cook the aubergine slices, in batches, for 2 minutes on each side, until golden. Remove and place on kitchen paper. Repeat to cook all of the aubergine. Pour off all but 1 tablespoon of oil from the frying pan, add the onion and garlic and cook for 2–3 minutes, stirring often. Add the tomatoes, basil and red wine, 250 ml water, season to taste and bring to the boil. Boil for 10 minutes, until you have a thickened sauce. Stir in the aubergine then add to the pasta, stirring well to combine.

Put the mixture in a large baking dish. Spoon the ricotta on top, sprinkle over the pecorino and bake in the preheated oven for 20 minutes until golden and crispy around the edges.

green lasagne with ricotta pesto and mushrooms

250 g fresh spinach lasagne sheets

mushroom sauce

25 g dried porcini mushrooms, soaked in warm water for 20 minutes

4 tablespoons olive oil

50 g unsalted butter

1 kg fresh wild mushrooms or portobellos, thinly sliced

1 onion, chopped

4 garlic cloves, chopped

4 tablespoons chopped flat leaf parsley

2–3 sprigs of thyme, chopped

300 ml chicken or vegetable stock

ricotta pesto

3 garlic cloves

75 g pine nuts

75 g basil leaves

150 ml olive oil

75 g unsalted butter, softened, plus extra to finish

4 tablespoons freshly grated Parmesan cheese, plus extra for sprinkling

200 g fresh ricotta cheese

sea salt and freshly ground black pepper

a baking dish, about 30 x 20 cm

SERVES 6

This colourful lasagne is sure to impress vegetarians and meat-eaters alike. It's good for entertaining as you can let it bake while chatting to your guests.

Preheat the oven to 180°C (350°F) Gas 4.

To make the sauce, drain the soaked mushrooms, reserving the liquid. Squeeze them gently, then chop coarsely. Heat half the oil and all the butter in a large frying pan. When foaming, add half the fresh and chopped dried mushrooms and half the onion. Fry over high heat for 4–5 minutes until tender. Repeat with the remaining mushrooms and onions, then combine in the pan. Stir in the garlic and herbs and cook for 2 minutes. Add the stock and soaking liquid, then boil for 4–5 minutes until syrupy. Leave to cool.

To make the pesto, pound the garlic, pine nuts and salt with a mortar and pestle. Add the basil leaves, a few at a time, pounding to a paste. Gradually beat in the olive oil until creamy. Beat in the butter, season with pepper, then beat in the Parmesan. Alternatively, put everything in a food processor and blend until smooth. Transfer to a bowl, add the ricotta, and stir well.

Bring a large saucepan of salted water to the boil and drop in a few lasagne sheets at a time. Fresh pasta is cooked when the water returns to the boil. Lift it out and drain over the sides of a colander. If using dried lasagne, follow the instructions on the packet.

Lightly oil the baking dish then line with a layer of lasagne and add a layer of ricotta pesto. Add another layer of pasta, a layer of mushroom sauce, then a layer of lasagne. Repeat, finishing with a layer of lasagne. Sprinkle with Parmesan and dot with butter.

Cover with oiled kitchen foil and bake in the preheated oven for 20 minutes. Uncover, then bake for a further 20 minutes until golden. Let stand for 10 minutes before serving.

This version of cannelloni combines a creamy sharp ricotta filling, speckled with slightly bitter green leaves and a sweet tomato sauce. The contrast in flavours between the sauce and filling is delicious.

cannelloni with ricotta, bitter greens and cherry tomato sauce

3 tablespoons olive oil

2 garlic cloves, finely chopped

750 g cherry tomatoes, halved

3 tablespoons chopped basil

100 g bitter salad greens such as rocket, watercress or spinach

500 g ricotta cheese

2 medium eggs, beaten

100 g freshly grated Parmesan cheese

freshly grated nutmeg, to taste

12 dried cannelloni tubes, 12 sheets fresh or dried lasagne or 1 recipe Fresh Egg Pasta (see page 12)

sea salt and freshly ground black pepper

a piping bag with a large plain nozzle

a baking dish, about 30 x 20 cm

SERVES 4–6

Preheat the oven to 200°C (400°F) Gas 6.

To make the tomato sauce, heat the oil in a saucepan, add the garlic and cook until just turning golden. Add the halved tomatoes. They should hiss as they go in – this will slightly caramelize the juices, and concentrate the flavour. Stir well, then simmer for 10 minutes. Stir in the basil and season with salt and pepper (the sauce should still appear quite lumpy). Set aside.

To make the ricotta filling, plunge the salad greens into a saucepan of boiling water for 1 minute, then drain well, squeezing out any excess moisture. Chop finely. Press the ricotta through a sieve into a bowl. Beat in the eggs, then add the chopped greens and half the Parmesan. Season with nutmeg, salt and pepper. Set aside.

Cook the cannelloni or lasagne sheets in a large saucepan of boiling salted water according to the packet instructions. If using homemade pasta, cook for 1 minute. Lift out of the water and drain on a clean tea towel.

Spoon the ricotta filling into the piping bag. Fill each tube of cannelloni or pipe down the shorter edge of each lasagne sheet and roll it up. Arrange the filled cannelloni tightly together in a single layer in a lightly oiled baking dish. Spoon over the tomato sauce and sprinkle with the remaining Parmesan.

Bake in the preheated oven for 25–30 minutes until bubbling. Serve immediately.

gourmet macaroni cheese

Mac and cheese is a firm comfort food favourite. Here it is given a modern makeover with gourmet cheeses like mascarpone and Parmesan, and a touch of garlic. The crisp topping rounds out the texture, making it live up to its name.

60 g fresh, chunky breadcrumbs

1 tablespoon olive oil

2 tablespoons butter

1 garlic clove, finely chopped

1 teaspoon dry mustard

3 tablespoons plain flour

500 ml milk

125 ml mascarpone

130 g grated mature Cheddar cheese

60 g grated Parmesan cheese

350 g rigatoni or macaroni

sea salt and freshly ground black pepper

a baking dish, 21 x 21 cm, or 4 ramekins

SERVES 4

Preheat the oven to 200°C (400°F) Gas 6.

Spread the breadcrumbs on a baking sheet, drizzle with the oil and season. Bake for 6 minutes, remove and set aside.

Melt the butter in a medium saucepan. Add the garlic and mustard and fry for 1 minute before adding the flour. Whisk constantly over medium heat until it forms a paste. Gradually whisk in the milk and turn up the heat. Bring to the boil, whisking constantly. Turn the heat down to low and simmer for 10 minutes. Remove from the heat and add the mascarpone, Cheddar and half of the Parmesan.

Boil the pasta in salted water until just al dente, drain and mix with the cheese sauce. Season and spoon the mixture into the baking dish or ramekins. Top with the breadcrumbs and the remaining Parmesan. Bake for 20 minutes until golden. Leave to sit for 5 minutes before serving.

index

recipe credits

Fiona Beckett
Aubergine and
  sausage rigatoni
  with red wine
Chicken tonnato salad

Maxine Clark
Dried pasta types
Making, flavouring and
  cooking pasta
Cannelloni with ricotta,
  bitter greens and
  cherry tomato sauce
Green lasagne with
  ricotta pesto and
  mushrooms
Ricotta, basil and
  · cherry tomato
  cannelloni
Spaghetti and prawns
  with pesto, cooked
  in a paper bag
Tagliolini with lemon
  and green olives
Walnut and caper pesto

Ross Dobson
Asparagus tagliatelle
Baked ziti with
  aubergine, basil
  and ricotta
Farfalle pasta with
  asparagus, soft-
  boiled duck eggs
  and Parmesan
Linguine with garlic
  and chilli clams
Linguine with heirloom
  tomatoes, red endive
  and black olives
Mushroom and thyme
  ragu with hand-torn
  pasta
Pappardelle with
  Portobello
  mushrooms
Pappardelle with roast
  fennel, tomato and
  olives
Penne with chilli
  meatballs
Pepper, olive and feta
  pasta salad
Smoky chorizo and

prawn gnocchetti
Spaghetti with broccoli,
  walnuts and ricotta
Spaghetti with
  butternut squash,
  sage and pecorino
Spaghetti with chilli
  courgette crumbs
Tagliatelle with pan-
  fried pumpkin and
  red pepper oil
Tuna, chilli and rocket
  pasta salad with feta
Wild mushroom lasagne

Clare Ferguson
Pappardelle with basil
  oil
Pappardelle with
  seafood sauce
Penne with mozzarella
  and tomatoes

Silvana Franco
Broccoli and pine nut
  pesto
Classic bolognese
Classic lasagne
Conchigliette soup
Crab tortellini
Creamy smoked
  salmon sauce
Creamy vodka sauce
Fusilli with salsa verde
  and chargrilled
  cheese
Ham and mushroom
  mezzalune
Herby steak sauce
Herbed tagliatelle with
  prawn skewers
Mussels in white wine
  with linguine
Oven-roasted spicy
  macaroni
Pancetta and chicken
  meatballs
Parma ham, rocket and
  bubbling blue cheese
Parsley and pancetta
  cannelloni
Pasta e fagioli
Pasta vongole
Pork and parmesan

ravioli
Roasted aubergine and
  tomato sauce
Roasted pumpkin with
  sage, lemon and
  mozzarella butter
Summer minestrone
Three cheese baked
  penne
Tomato sauce with
  double basil

Tonia George
Italian meatballs with
  tomato sauce and
  spaghetti
Pappardelle with
  breaded chicken
  and garlic-parsley
  butter
Pork and lemon ragu
Tagliatelle with peas
  and goats' cheese
  pesto

Brian Glover
Pasta with courgette,
  mint, lemon and
  cream
Pasta with mussels,
  prawns, lemon and
  garlic
Pasta with pan-fried
  squash, walnut and
  parsley sauce

Nicola Graimes
Linguine with prawns,
  peas and lemon
Pancetta and bean
  rigatoni
Tagliatelle with sun-
  blush tomatoes and
  toasted pine nuts

Jennifer Joyce
Gourmet macaroni
  cheese

Caroline Marson
Artichoke and almond
  pesto
Coriander, chilli and
  peanut pesto
Mint, ginger and
  almond pesto
Red pepper and walnut

pesto
Tagliatelle with broccoli,
  anchovies, parmesan
  and crème fraîche

Louise Pickford
Chilli tuna tartare pasta
Fishmarket sauce
Foaming sage butter
Gorgonzola, pecan and
  mascarpone sauce
Lemon and vermouth
  sauce
Pasta with fresh tomato
Pasta with melted
  ricotta and herby
  parmesan sauce
Pesto
Roasted squash, feta
  and sage sauce
Roasted tomato sauce
Sausage ragu
Slow-roasted tomatoes
  with ricotta and
  spaghetti
Tapenade

Fiona Smith
Lemon-rubbed lamb
  and orzo salad
Pea, prosciutto and
  pasta salad

Fran Warde
Chicken and tarragon
  pesto pasta
Ham and pea fusilli
Macaroni, spinach and
  cheese bake
Tossed courgette
  ribbons and pasta

Laura Washburn
Linguine with peas,
  pancetta and sage

Lindy Wildsmith
Pairing sauces with
  pasta
Aglio, olio e
  peperoncino
Amatriciana
Basic cream sauce
  with butter and
  parmesan
Béchamel sauce with
  prosciutto, emmental

and salad leaves
Calabrese and broccoli
  arabesque
Chilli and black bean
  sauce with garlic-
  fried breadcrumbs
Country sausage, peas
  and tomatoes
Courgette and toasted
  pine nut pasta
Ligurian meat sauce
Monkfish and italian
  vegetables with
  olives and capers
Mushroom cream
  sauce with garlic,
  parsley and marsala

Pasta primavera
Penne with
  mascarpone, spinach
  and pancetta
Pot luck summer pasta
Prawns and salmon
  with a citrus cream
  sauce
Puttanesca
Ricotta, cinnamon and
  walnut sauce
Roasted vegetable
  sauce with capers
  and cherry tomatoes
Spaghetti alla carbonara
Tuna and coriander
  pasta salad

photography credits

Caroline Arber
Pages 7 centre, 64,
225

Martin Brigdale
Pages 2, 4, 17, 19, 41,
53, 58, 161, 184, 193,
203, 210, 218, 234

Peter Cassidy
Pages 3, 8, 12, 13 all,
14 all, 16, 26, 35, 46,
69, 77, 81, 84, 85, 89,
90, 91, 98, 108, 111,
113, 123, 127, 157, 165,
170, 192, 201, 207,
209, 230, 233

Nicki Dowey
Pages 7 above, 10
below, 29, 40, 47, 60,
83, 88, 121, 126, 130,
134, 137, 145, 175,
180, 188, 208

Richard Jung
Pages 30, 104, 115,
116, 117, 129, 138, 142,
149, 150, 152, 153,
154, 164, 173, 186,
191, 194, 226, 227, 229

William Lingwood
Pages 1, 7 below, 10

above all, 20, 21, 22,
25, 44, 51, 52, 59, 67,
71, 75, 80, 87, 92, 96,
100, 103, 118, 125,
133, 166, 172, 176,
179, 199, 200, 213,
214, 217, 221, 223, 228

Diana Miller
Pages 31, 33, 38, 68,
128, 143

David Munns
Pages 5, 9, 182, 183,
235

Noel Murphy
Pages 196, 222

William Reavell
Pages 48, 55, 72, 79,
95, 122, 139, 171

Debi Treloar
Pages 45, 76, 141

Ian Wallace
Pages 6, 11, 37, 63,
106, 107, 114, 158, 162,
187, 195, 204, 211

Kate Whitaker
Pages 18, 34, 43, 56,
99, 110, 146